Strategic Studies Institute
and
U.S. Army War College Press

COUNTERING RADICALIZATION
AND RECRUITMENT TO AL-QAEDA:
FIGHTING THE WAR OF DEEDS

Paul Kamolnick

June 2014

*****

Comments pertaining to this report are invited and should be forwarded to: Director, Strategic Studies Institute and U.S. Army War College Press, U.S. Army War College, 47 Ashburn Drive, Carlisle, PA 17013-5010.

*****

This manuscript was funded by the U.S. Army War College External Research Associates Program. Information on this program is available on our website, *www.StrategicStudies Institute.army.mil*, at the Opportunities tab.

*****

*****

The Strategic Studies Institute and U.S. Army War College Press publishes a monthly email newsletter to update the national security community on the research of our analysts, recent and forthcoming publications, and upcoming conferences sponsored by the Institute. Each newsletter also provides a strategic commentary by one of our research analysts. If you are interested in receiving this newsletter, please subscribe on the SSI website at *www.StrategicStudiesInstitute.army.mil/newsletter*.

FOREWORD

Twenty-five years after al-Qaeda's founding, countering al-Qaeda radicalization and recruitment remains a key U.S. Government (USG) strategic objective. Al-Qaeda proclaims itself **the** true Islamic vanguard seeking to overthrow alleged anti-Muslim apostate governments throughout the Arab Muslim world. Conducting spectacular, carefully orchestrated anti-Western mass casualty terrorist attacks as a component of a broader pan-Sunni Islamist insurgent strategy, al-Qaeda deftly employs insidious propaganda. This propaganda creates Manichean alternatives—"The Crusader-Zionist War Against Islam" versus "The Vanguard Defender of the Muslim Umma"—that have not been decisively discredited despite a barrenness in fact. An underground of self-radicalizing individuals and small cliques incited by al-Qaeda agitation propaganda now also occupies the attention of the intelligence and criminal justice sectors of virtually every Western nation.

USG officials charged with counterterrorist messaging have yet to effectively counter al-Qaeda's information warfare. The reasons for this, and a proposed methodology for rectifying it, are the core themes of Dr. Paul Kamolnick's monograph. First, he argues that we have failed as a nation to realize fully that deeds are the most potent communication. Second, that many of our policies, actions, and deeds incite anger, moral indignation, outrage, and even hate in regions of the Arab and Muslim world most vulnerable to our nation's least palatable foreign and military policies. This failure to view the world through Arab and Muslim eyes, Kamolnick asserts, has enabled al-Qaeda's sophisticated insurgent propaganda to successfully rationalize a violent strategy to assault what it alleges are those apostate pillars enabling Western hegemony in its Crusader War against a besieged and oppressed Muslim faith. Third, Kamolnick provides a highly critical review of several official reports and analyses proposing various remedial messaging strategies to "Sell America to a Westernized secular elite." It is unlikely, he argues, that U.S. credibility in the Arab and Muslim world can be enhanced through diplomatic spin, empty platitudes, vague pronouncements, or in his words, "putting lipstick on pigs." This strategy he claims, whether disingenuous or simply unimaginative, has failed and will to continue do so.

The USG's substantial credibility deficit is the proximate cause enabling al-Qaeda's information warfare advantage. Kamolnick's counterintuitive conclusion, however, is that, while the USG does maintain certain questionable alliances, exhibit a penchant for regime stability, and maintain a strategy of forward deployment in defense of vital energy corridors—succinctly summarized by him as "oil, Israel, and autocracy"—al-Qaeda can produce **no** evidence that the USG in deeds, policies, or actions is a religious Crusader bent on extirpating Islam. Indeed, authoritative polling suggests substantial majorities in the Arab and Muslim world highly rank many core American values and distinguish between overall favorable attitudes toward America and Americans, and often vehement opposition to certain American foreign and military policies. Moreover, highly reputed militant Islamists are on record stating that U.S. strategic interests do not preclude seeking and finding common ground on a range of key issues of great concern to the Islamic world.

Having made the case for taking USG deeds seriously, Kamolnick shifts to proposing and outlining a methodology for leveraging the power of deeds against al-Qaeda. He first offers a conceptualization of adversary propaganda as a component of what he calls the insurgent "terrorist quadrangle" comprising political objectives, terrorist propaganda, terrorist actions, and strategic objectives. He then provides a detailed outline of those core themes and messages which, if systematically organized in a coherent sustained information counteroffensive, undermine al-Qaeda's case for employing terroristic violence. Key to this campaign is that al-Qaeda's own deeds serve as the most damning evidence of its actual status as a criminal terrorist organization waging a self-declared offensive war to impose its will through terror on all — Muslim and non-Muslim — who disagree. Specifically, al-Qaeda's perfidious methods, terroristic modus operandi, and responsibility for besmirching the Islamic Call, prove that it forsakes the shari'a of lawful jihad and is guilty of the commission of major sins in Islam; undermines Islamic and Muslim interests; and that its signature methods of coercion, force, and fear deny the rightful autonomy of persons — Muslim and non-Muslim — to exercise essential political and civil rights.

Why a War of Deeds conceived in the manner Kamolnick suggests has not been operationalized in official USG strategy is puzzling. If he is right, it certainly does appear that al-Qaeda's center of gravity as self-proclaimed vanguard and defender of a besieged Umma is vulnerable to frontal assault by the powers of reason, fact, and the evidence of deeds. This monograph provides much food for thought. Though provocative and in places possibly controversial, its argument deserves the serious attention of USG personnel tasked with conceptualizing and executing an effective information warfare strategy to counter this lethal adversary.

Douglas C. Lovelace

DOUGLAS C. LOVELACE, JR.
Director
Strategic Studies Institute and
    U.S. Army War College Press

ABOUT THE AUTHOR

PAUL KAMOLNICK is full professor of sociology in the Department of Sociology and Anthropology, East Tennessee State University, USA. He teaches courses in classical and contemporary social theory, and the sociology of global terrorism. His primary research focus is developing theory and methods for countering radicalization and recruitment to Al-Qaeda Senior Leadership Endorsed (AQSLE) Anti-American terrorism. He is the author of *Delegitimizing Al-Qaeda: A Jihad-Realist Approach* (Carlisle, PA: Strategic Studies Institute, U.S. Army War College, March 2012), and has published counterterrorism-related articles and reviews in *Terrorism and Political Violence*, *Studies in Conflict and Terrorism*, *Perspectives on Terrorism*, and the *Small Wars Journal*. Dr. Kamolnick holds a Ph.D. from Florida State University, Tallahassee, Florida.

SUMMARY

Disrupting, dismantling, and ultimately defeating al-Qaeda-based, affiliated, and inspired terrorism is the declared policy of the U.S. Government (USG). Despite noteworthy success in attacking the al-Qaeda (AQ) terrorist network and securing the homeland from terrorist attack, the United States has yet to execute an effective methodology for countering radicalization and recruitment to AQ. This monograph proposes a distinct War of Deeds methodology for accomplishing this.

A War of Deeds is to be fought on two interrelated fronts: changing deeds and challenging deeds. Changing deeds requires a frank examination and possible reorienting of those present-day USG foreign, military, and diplomatic policies that diminish USG credibility and potentially enhance the resonance of AQ's terrorist propaganda in the Muslim world. It also requires a frank examination of existing USG information operations that in the opinion of the present writer fail to adequately address the present U.S. credibility deficit and whose proposals too often amount to unpersuasive marketing endeavors pitched to a highly selective Westernized audience.

Challenging deeds involves systematically, comprehensively, and forcefully countering AQ's terrorist propaganda, fabrications, and disinformation with verifiable facts. First, I undertake a careful analysis of the nature and function of propaganda in terrorist operations. I demonstrate the vital importance of AQ propaganda through the use of a proposed analytic construct—a "terrorist quadrangle"—linking political objectives, terrorist propaganda, terrorist acts, and strategic objectives; characterize the critical role and function of counterpropaganda in information warfare; and contrast counterpropaganda, as here defined, with current definitions of psychological operations (PSYOP) or military information support operations (MISO).

Next, I offer a comprehensive interpretation of influence operations, and a broadened conception of the nature of contemporary war and warfare. Here departing from the conventional seven instruments of national power captured by the Diplomatic, Information, Military, Economic, Financial, Intelligence and Law Enforcement (DIMEFIL) or Military, Information/Intelligence, Diplomatic, Legal, Infrastructure, Finance, and Economic (MIDLIFE) acronyms, I advance a new acronym, DICEFILM (Diplomatic, Informational, Cyber, Economic, Financial, Intelligence, Legal, Military), which explicitly incorporates the cyber dimension of warfare, increasing to eight the instruments of national power. After providing this broadened conception of influence operations, contemporary warfare, and instruments of national power, I outline and illustrate the War of Deeds methodology for countering AQ's messengers, media, and message; and demonstrate how this methodology may be used to counter the two "great lies" authorizing AQ's terrorist modus operandi, i.e., that the USG is an implacable foe and declared enemy of Islam and the greater Muslim world ("The Crusader"), and that al-Qaeda is fighting a purely defensive jihad on behalf of the oppressed worldwide Muslim faith community ("The Defender").

Following a brief conclusion, select strategic considerations are examined with focus especially on the potential suitability, acceptability, and risks accompanying a proposed War of Deeds.

COUNTERING RADICALIZATION AND RECRUITMENT TO AL-QAEDA: FIGHTING THE WAR OF DEEDS

In the propaganda pioneered by al-Qaeda, terrorism is merely self-defense against a perceived American war on Islam. There has been no more stark statement of this belief than the courtroom declarations of Mr. Faisal Shahzad as he pleaded guilty and was sentenced to life without parole for the failed bombing in Times Square, New York. Calling himself a 'Muslim soldier,' Mr. Shahzad denounced the wars in Afghanistan and Iraq and drone strikes in Pakistan and Yemen. The drones, he said, 'kill women, children, they kill everybody. . . . It's a war, and in war, they kill people,' he added. 'They're killing all Muslims.'[1]

Scott Shane
April 2013

We will continue to make it clear that the United States is not—and never will be—at war with Islam. We will focus on al-Qaeda's ability to project its message across a range of media, challenge the legitimacy and accuracy of the assertions and behavior it advances, and promote a greater understanding of U.S. policies and actions and an alternative to al-Qaeda's vision. We also will seek to amplify positive and influential messages that undermine the legitimacy of al-Qaeda's and its actions and contest its worldview. In some cases, we may convey our ideas and messages through person-to-person engagement, other times through the power of social media, and in every case through the message of our deeds.[2]

Barack H. Obama
President of the United States
June 2011

1

The arrest or death of existing terrorists will be only a short-term success if al-Qaeda continues to recruit, indoctrinate, and train new members successfully. The U.S. Government must therefore determine how it can dissuade new recruits from joining al-Qaeda, as well as discourage individuals from providing the terrorist organization financial and other support.[3]

Kim Cragin and Scott Gerwehr
2005

INTRODUCTION

In a previous monograph, the author proposed a distinct "jihad realist" approach for countering radicalization and recruitment to al-Qaeda (AQ).[4] It was argued that the military jihad is, and remains, a binding religious imperative for militant Islamists; a classical Islamic jurisprudence (*fiqh al-jihad*) regulates the waging of this military jihad; AQ's anti-American mass casualty terrorism substantially violates this jurisprudence; and that this orthodox classical Sunnite *fiqh al-jihad* can, and should, be leveraged to delegitimize AQ: especially among that sliver of recruits for whom upholding the shari'a is paramount, and the avoidance of major sins is a moral imperative.

The present monograph proposes a "War of Deeds" to supplement the author's jihad-realist approach. Its intended target audience comprises many different types of morally outraged potential recruits influenced by AQ's terrorist propaganda that (self-) radicalize and (self-) recruit to "homegrown" and "home-based" terrorism or foreign theaters of conflict. This War of Deeds is to be fought on two interrelated fronts: changing deeds and challenging deeds.

Changing deeds requires a frank examination and possible reorienting of those present-day U.S. Govern-

2

ment (USG) foreign, military, and diplomatic policies that diminish USG credibility in the Muslim world, and also potentially enhance the resonance of AQ's terrorist propaganda.

Challenging deeds involves systematically, comprehensively, and forcefully countering AQ's terrorist propaganda, fabrications, and disinformation with verifiable facts.

A key premise of the present monograph is that, despite recognition that USG policies and actions are key drivers of attitudes and perceptions in the wider Muslim world, this recognition of deeds **as** communication has yet to inform sufficiently present terrorist countermessaging strategy. To put it another way, if what we **do** matters far more than what we **say**, or what we say about what we do; if **policies and actions** speak far louder than **words**; if **actions**, not **platitudes**, signify definitive proof of one's motives; then, this premise is neither fully acknowledged nor systematically exploited in USG information warfare designed to counter and delegitimize AQ's terrorist propaganda.

That the USG need not be beyond moral reproach or innocent of superpower capacities, interests, or behaviors, is a second, albeit counterintuitive, premise, anchoring the present argument. Ironically, this makes a systematic War of Deeds a more productive **and** candid endeavor. How so? USG veracity, credibility, and **not** moral perfection of motives or deeds is key. The USG's dirtiest laundry discloses **at worst** that it engages in superpower *realpolitik*, privileges specific alliances, and defends what it perceives to be its vital strategic interests in an imperfect world using imperfect means. Evidence **does not** support a case however, even remotely, that the USG is leading or fomenting a Crusader alliance against Islam. Yes, one can discover evidence for genuine tractable clashes of interests, intra-civilizational fault lines over religion and state, and even inter-civilizational dialogue and conflict; however, again, there is **no credible evidence** of a Crusader War against Islam or any systematic animus directed against Islam or Muslims in general. I have said nothing of the USG's cleaner laundry, and there is much of it. I have said nothing of AQ's dirtiest laundry, and there is much of that, described in appropriate context as the argument unfolds. A detailed outline of the argument follows.

First, data is reviewed confirming AQ's continuing resilience, and also noting progress, or lack thereof, toward accomplishing declared USG policy and its three key strategic objectives outlined in the *9/11 Commission Report* (2004). Second, it is asserted that USG policies, deeds, and actions **are** communication, that they affect message resonance in the Arab and Muslim world, and the two key fronts in a proposed War of Deeds are identified: changing deeds, and challenging deeds.

Third, a detailed examination of the first front, changing deeds, is provided. I first examine select efforts in USG public diplomacy and their relative failure to put "lipstick on pigs." I assess the unique challenges and opportunities arising from current USG foreign and military policies. Then I assert the vital importance of AQ tactical propaganda in relation to this author's proposed analytic construct—a "terrorist quadrangle"— linking political objectives, terrorist propaganda, terrorist acts, and strategic objectives; characterize the critical role and function of counter-propaganda in information warfare. Finally, I contrast counterpropaganda as here defined, with current definitions of psychological operations (PSYOP).

In the remainder of the monograph, I outline, describe, and defend key elements comprising the second front: challenging deeds in a USG counter-propaganda counteroffensive against AQ. I begin by proposing a comprehensive interpretation of influence operations, and a broadened conception of the nature of contemporary war and warfare. Second, departing from the conventional seven instruments of national power captured by the Diplomatic, Information, Military, Economic, Financial, Intelligence and Law Enforcement (DIMEFIL) or Military, Information/Intelligence, Diplomatic, Legal, Infrastructure, Finance, and Economic (MIDLIFE) acronyms, I advance a new acronym, DICEFILM (Diplomatic, Informational, Cyber, Economic, Financial, Intelligence, Legal, Military) which explicitly incorporates the cyber dimension of warfare, increasing to eight the instruments of national power.

Third, after providing this broadened conception of influence operations, contemporary warfare, and instruments of national power, I assert the primacy of a War of Deeds for challenging AQ's terrorist propaganda. I outline and illustrate the War of Deeds methodology for countering AQ's messengers, media, and message. I demonstrate how this methodology may be used to counter the two "great lies" authorizing AQ's terrorist modus operandi, i.e., that the USG is an implacable foe and declared enemy of Islam and the greater Muslim world ("The Crusader"); and that AQ is fighting a purely **defensive** jihad on behalf of the oppressed worldwide Muslim faith community ("The Defender"). In conclusion, I summarize the main themes of the previous argument and offer concrete suggestions for strategists tasked with countering radicalization and recruitment to AQ.

AL QAEDA: AN EVOLVING THREAT, POLICY, AND STRATEGY

Despite declared USG policy to disrupt, dismantle, and ultimately defeat AQ,[5] AQ and its affiliates, allies, and those motivated and inspired by its vision, continue to pose a significant threat to American citizens and U.S. national security. A decade of sanguine declarations and commentary predicting AQ's decline, demise, or even strategic defeat[6] have been repeatedly upstaged by this resilient and highly adaptive enemy, and more "bearish" assessments have proven more reliable.[7] AQ's persistence as a lethal global threat—despite the May 2, 2011, killing of Osama bin Laden[8]—and the August 2013 USG closure of nearly two dozen U.S. embassy compounds and worldwide travel alert,[9] furnish additional evidence for this bearish view. In addition, AQ, either directly or more generally through tactical allies, affiliates, or terrorist acts carried out in its name is associated with a lethal swath of global terrorist incidents. In 2011, 11 of the top 20 most active terrorist groups were linked to AQ. Together, those groups carried out over 780 attacks, resulting in 3,000 deaths and more than 4,600 wounded. Further, four of the five most lethal attacks were linked to an AQ-linked group (AQ in the Arabian Peninsula [AQAP], Tehrik-i-Taliban Pakistan, al-Shabaab, and AQ in Iraq).[10] In 2012, six of the top 10 terrorist perpetrator groups worldwide had at least limited association with AQ's global insurgent terrorist modus operandi, conducting 1,470 terrorist attacks, which resulted in 4,938 deaths.[11]

Recent reports documenting how AQ's encrypted cyber communication facilitates transnational terrorist logistics and organization further evidences the adaptive capacities of this lethal adversary.[12] Finally, USG recognition of the evolving AQ threat ensures that strategists will be tasked with developing effective methods for countering this resilient foe. [13]

THREE STRATEGIC OBJECTIVES

The seminal *9/11 Commission* Report (2004) identifies three key strategic objectives for a comprehensive counter-AQ strategy: (1) attacking terrorists and their organizations; (2) preventing the continued growth of Islamist terrorism; and, (3) protecting against and preparing for terrorist attacks.[14] Progress on two of these three strategic objectives, attacking terrorists and their organizations and protecting against and preparing for terrorist attacks, has certainly contributed to preventing successful mass-casualty terrorist attacks on the scale of September 11, 2001 (9/11).

Attacking Terrorists and Their Organizations.

Defeating the AQ terrorist entity necessitates systematically attacking, degrading, and ultimately destroying its means of sustaining itself as an ongoing organizational enterprise. Military, diplomatic, financial, legal, and intelligence instruments of national power have been deployed to great effect to accomplish the following: identify and prioritize sanctuary denial, actual or potential, in free states, failing states, and remote regions; attack terrorists and their organizations via identification, disruption, capture, and kill; attack elements required for complex international terrorist operation, including time, space, the ability to plan, and presence of a functional command structure; constrain the opportunity and space to recruit, train, and select operatives; attack and deny logistics networks; deny access to weapons of mass destruction (WMD) elements; disrupt reliable communication; and, eliminate the ability and opportunity for pre-testing planning.[15]

National Counterterrorism Center (NCTC) Director Matthew Olsen directly references these elements when, in congressional testimony, he delineated accomplishments against AQ during the period under review (August 2011-2012):

> [W]e have made significant progress in the fight against terrorism. Our nation has placed relentless pressure on al-Qa'ida's leadership. We have denied the group safe havens, resources, and the ability to plan and train. Following the death last year of Usama bin Ladin, several of his top lieutenants have been eliminated. The leaders that remain lack experience and are under siege. They have limited ability to recruit and communicate with other operatives. In short, the intelligence picture shows that al-Qa'ida core is a shadow of its former self, and the overall threat from al-Qa'ida in Pakistan is diminished. Further, the government has disrupted terrorist attacks in the United States and abroad. Our intelligence officers have worked diligently to identify and stop terrorist plots before they are executed. And we have investigated and prosecuting [sic] individuals who have sought to carry out and supported [sic] terrorist operations.[16]

James R. Clapper, Director of National Intelligence (DNI), also references this strategic objective when he states in reference to "core AQ": "Senior personnel losses in 2012, amplifying losses and setbacks since 2008, have degraded core AQ to a point that the group is probably unable to carry out complex, large-scale attacks in the West." He continues, however,

8

The group has essentially the same strategic goals since its initial declaration of war against the United States in 1996, and to the extent that the group endures, its leaders will not abandon the aspiration to attack inside the United States.[17]

Finally, in his May 23, 2013, National Defense University (NDU) speech, "The Future of our Fight Against Terrorism," outlining and defending his proposed counter-terrorist policy and strategy states specifically in relation to targeting terrorists, President Barack Obama stated:

> After I took office, we stepped up the war against al Qaeda, but also sought to change its course. We relentlessly targeted al Qaeda's leadership. Today, Osama bin Laden is dead, and so are most of his top lieutenants. There have been no large-scale attacks on the United States, and our homeland is more secure. Today, the core of al Qaeda in Afghanistan and Pakistan is on a path to defeat. Their remaining operatives spend more time thinking about their own safety than plotting against us. They did not direct the attacks in Benghazi or Boston. They have not carried out a successful attack on our homeland since 9/11.[18]

The USG Policy of Targeted Killing of High Value Targets (HVTs) Using Armed Unmanned Aerial Vehicles (UAVs, or "Drones"). Apprehending, arresting, and incarcerating AQ terrorists has been pursued,[19] and Special Forces raids carried out to find, fix, and finish specific targets, including on May 2, 2011, AQ emir Osama bin Laden. Undoubtedly, the targeted killing of HVTs using UAVs or "drones" has been the dominant tactic of choice to disrupt, dismantle, and defeat AQ. After describing the Abbottabad, Pakistan raid leading to the killing of Osama bin Laden, President Obama forthrightly stated his rationale for a policy of targeted killing:

> It is . . . not possible for America to simply deploy a team of Special Forces to capture every terrorist. And even when such an approach may be possible, there are places where it would pose profound risks to our troops and local civilians– where a terrorist compound cannot be breached without triggering a firefight with surrounding tribal communities that pose no threat to us, or when putting U.S. boots on the ground may trigger a major international crisis. . . . To put it another way, our operation in Pakistan against Osama bin Laden cannot be the norm. The risks in that case were immense; the likelihood of capture, although our preference, was remote given the certainty of resistance; the fact that we did not find ourselves confronted with civilian casualties, or embroiled in an extended firefight, was a testament to the meticulous planning and professionalism of our Special Forces— but also depended on some luck. . . . And even then, the cost to our relationship with Pakistan—and the backlash among the Pakistani public over encroachment on their territory—was so severe that we are just now beginning to rebuild this important partnership. . . . It is in this context that the United States has taken lethal, targeted action against al Qaeda and its associated forces, including with remotely piloted aircraft commonly referred to as drones.[20]

Evidence in support of the suitability/efficacy of drones for finding, fixing, and finishing terrorist HVTs is compelling,[21] as is their lawfulness as a tool of war.[22] This likely explains recent trends in the expansion of drone bases whether used primarily for surveillance, lethal targeting, or both,[23] as well as more recent official pronouncements.[24]

The following evidence corroborates this assertion. The drone campaign largely focused on the North and South Waziristan regions in Pakistan has devastated key AQ-based leadership and operatives, and key anti-USG forces attacking USG and Coalition International Security Assistance Forces (ISAF). Between 2004 and November 29, 2013, 353 strikes had been conducted, with 342 taking place since January 2008, with the number of casualties as follows: in 2006 (122), 2007 (73), 2008 (286), 2009 (463), 2010 (801), 2011 (405), 2012 (300), and 2013 (119 as of November 29, 2013). Of those 353 strikes, 72 percent have hit targets in North Waziristan, and 24 percent have hit targets in South Waziristan. The number of Taliban/AQ leaders killed in the territories of various Taliban factions from 2004-13 include the territory of Abu Kasha al Iraqi (12), The Haqqani Network (14), Mullah Nazir (9), Mehsud (7), Hafiz Gul Bahadar (6), Faqir Mohammed (2), and Gulbuddin Hekmatyar (1).[25] The New America Foundation records the following totals for the 2004 to November 21, 2013, time frame: total drone strikes at 369; total numbers killed at 2,077-3,424, and the total number of militants killed at 1,620-2,783.[26]

More telling, however, is the data for HVTs removed from the field of battle. The total numbers include 1 in 2004, 2 in 2005, 2 in 2006, 0 in 2007, 19 in 2008, 18 in 2009, 20 in 2010, 9 in 2011, 13 in 2012, and 19 as of November 23, 2013.[27] Consider the following select examples:

- Senior-level clerics and ideologues: Abu Yahya al Libi,[28] Kahlid bin Abdul Rahman al Husainan, Mansur al Shami;

- Trainers: Abu Saif al Jaziri, Abdullah Hamas al Filistini, Abu Musa al Masri, Abu Rashid, Muhammaed Ilyas Kuwaiti, Muhammad Sajid Yamani;
- Commanders: Abu Laith al Libi, Khalid Habib, Abdullah Said al Libi, Hazrat Omar, Khan Mohammed, Sheikh Yasin al Kuwaiti;
- Financiers: Mustafa Abu Yazid and Abu Zaid al Iraqi;
- Bomb makers and explosives experts, including WMD: Abu Hamza and Abu Khabab al Masri;
- Faciliators: Abdullah Azzam al Saudi;
- Intelligence chiefs: Abu Ubaydah Abdullah al Adam;
- External operations senior operatives or chiefs to West and other regions: Abu Sulayman Jazairi, Abu Jihad al Masri, Osama al Kini, Saleh al Somali, Sadam Hussein al Hussami, Osama bin Ali bin Abdullah bin Damjan al Dawasari, Abu Hafs al Shahri, Aslam Awan;
- Suicide operations chiefs: Wali Mohammed;
- High-level leaders: Hakimullah Mehsud, Baitullah Mehsud, Tahir Yuldashev, Sheikh Fateh al Masri, Jan Baz Zadran, Mullah Sangeen Zadran, Abd al Rahman al Yemeni, Abu Miqdad al Masri, Badr Mansoor, Abu Usamn Adil, Abu Yahya al Libi, Mullah Nazir, Attah Ullah Rafy Khan, and Waliur Rehman.[29]

Of extreme value has been the removal of AQ's operatives who have previously become global managers:
- Abu Faraj al Libi, from 2001 until capture in Pakistan in May 2005;

- Mustafa Abu al Yazid, (aka: Sheikh Saeed), 2005 until death by drone strike in May 2010;
- Atiyah Abd al Rahman, 2010 until death by drone strike August 22, 2011; and
- Abu Yahya al Libi, 2011 until death by drone strike June 2012.[30]

Seven key AQ leaders were killed by drone strikes in Pakistan subsequent to the May 2, 2011, Special Forces operation that led to the killing of AQ emir Osama bin Laden:

- Abu Yahya al-Libi;
- Ilyas Kashmiri (head of AQ's military and member of external operations council);
- Atiyah abd al Rahman (bin Laden's former chief of staff and Zawahiri's previous deputy);
- Abu Miqdad al Masri (a member of AQ's Shura Majlis also involved in external operations);
- Badr Mansoor (AQ leader in Pakistan and key link to the Taliban and Pakistani jihadist groups);
- Aslam Awan (deputy to the leader of AQ external operations); and,
- Abu Hafs al Shahri (senior AQ leader and operations chief for Pakistan).

The role of drones in attacking AQ's lethal affiliate, the Yemeni-based AQAP, is similarly telling. The number of U.S. airstrikes in Yemen climbed from under five per year from 2002-10 to 10 in 2011, 42 in 2012, and 24 as of December 9, 2013. The number of AQAP casualties was 81 in 2011, 193 in 2012, and 97 as of December 9, 2013.[31]

The USG-targeted killing of American-born Yemeni Anwar al-Awlaki, senior AQAP leader, propagandist, and religious figure, in a drone strike in Yemen on September 30, 2011, is one of the more notable strategic successes of the ongoing drone campaign in Yemen. Killed in Marib in the Province of Jawf, Awlaki was considered, "Al Qaeda's greatest English-language propagandist and one of its top operational planners."[32] Awlaki's deadly reach is especially evident in the plots he helped plan and persons he inspired to attack in the United States. According to Peter Bergen:

> 24 'homegrown' violent jihadist extremists in the United States who have been indicted or convicted of terrorism or have been killed while engaged in violent jihad since 2001 read Awlaki's propaganda or maintained contact with him.[33]

Some of the most notorious of those inspired by Awlaki to perpetrate or attempt to perpetrate the mass-killing of Americans, include:

- Army Major Nidal Malik Hasan, MD, age 39, Army psychiatrist, recently convicted and sentenced to death on April 15, 2013, for the November 5, 2009, shooting and murder at Fort Hood, TX, of 13 soldiers, and wounding 31.
- Umar Farouk Abdulmutallab, age 25, who pled guilty to eight charges, including attempted murder and terrorism, for the December 25, 2009, failed "underwear" bombing aimed at downing Northwest Airlines Flight 253 carrying 279 passengers and 11 crew members as it approached Detroit, MI.[34]
- Zachary Adam Chesser (aka Abu Talha al-Amerikee) age 25, sentenced February 24, 2011, to serve 25 years in federal prison for three felony charges: providing material support to

terrorists, communicating threats, and soliciting others to commit violence.[35]

- Najibullah Zazi, for the September 2009 attempted suicide attack in New York's subway system.
- Pakistani-American Faisal Shahzad, age 35, for the failed May 1, 2010, vehicle-born improvised explosive device (VIED) deployed in Times Square, New York, now serving a mandatory life sentence for his guilty plea on 10 felony counts.
- Carlos Leon Bledsoe (aka, Abdulhakim Muhammad), for the June 1, 2009, drive-by shooting and killing of a soldier outside a Little Rock, AR, military recruiting station, now serving a life sentence.[36]
- Dhokhar (age 19), and Tamerlan Tsarnaev (age 26), for having denotated two pressure cooker bombs during the Boston marathon, killing four (two females, aged 29 and 23; an 8-year old boy; and an MIT police officer, Sean A. Collier, killed three days after the bombing), and injuring 264 others, many seriously and requiring amputation, including the serious wounding of a Transit Police officer.

The present drone policy has disrupted a Mumbai-style mass casualty terror attack directed at Britain, France, and Germany[37] as well as efforts to acquire and operationalize WMD.[38] It has also disrupted the best of the terrorist bomb makers[39] and those senior operational leaders enganged in transmitting terror craft to other affiliates.[40] Finally, this drone policy has also disrupted long sought after chief facilitators, couriers, and operatives such as Mustafa Hajji Muham-

15

mad Khan (aka: Hassan Ghul).[41] It also likely presumes that the security of confinement and imprisonment in many nations is unpredictable,[42] and that, while highly desirable and necessary, existing "Rewards for Justice"[43] bounties placed on HVTs cannot supplant a surer way to find, fix, and finish declared enemies.

Many crucial HVTs are still at large and are certainly of intense interest to USG counterterrorism (CT) operators. For example:

- Dr. Ayman al-Zawahiri,[44] present AQ emir and life-long violent Islamist;
- Nasir Abdul Karim al-Wuhayshi, current emir of AQAP and now general manager and second in command in AQ;
- Khalid al-Habib, responsible for AQ operations in Afghanistan and northern Pakistan;
- Adnan el Shukrijumah and Saif al-Adel high-level AQ senior leaders;
- Mustafa Hamid, father-in-law of Saif al-Adel;
- Shaikh Said al-Sharif;
- Abu Mohammad al-Masri;
- Anas al-Libi;
- Matiur Rehman, a Pakistani militant and AQ planning chief;
- Abu Khalil al-Madani, senior AQ operative; and,
- Adam Gadahn, senior AQ communications and media official.

Also of intense value is Abdelmalek Droukdel (aka: Abu Musab Abdelwadoud), leader of al-Qaeda in the Islamic Magreb (AQIM), whose violent pedigree runs deep, his having joined the Algerian Islamic Group (GIA) in 1995, a splinter group, becoming a member of the GIA splinter group the Salafi Group for Preaching and Combat (GSPC) in 1998 — whose formal subordination to AQ was announced in 2003 — to becoming the emir of the GSPC in mid-2004, and after 2006 joining forces with AQ and in January 2007, changing its name to AQIM. Others include:

- Sirajuddin Haqqani, head of the Haqqani network;[45] and,
- Ibrahim Sulaiman al Rubaish, AQAP's mufti and a former Guantanamo Bay, Cuba, detainee.[46]

Protection Against and Preparation for Terrorist Attacks.

Protecting and preparing the U.S. homeland against terrorist attacks is a second key objective of current strategy.[47] The following chief elements were identified by the 9/11 Commission as essential to this objective:

- prohibiting terrorist travel;
- acquiring and deploying biometric screening systems;
- enhancing border security and immigration law enforcement;
- enhancing aviation and transportation security; creating a layered security system;
- setting priorities for national preparedness;
- ensuring that command, control, and communications are intact and operative following a terrorist attack;
- enhancing private sector preparedness; and,
- ensuring that American's civil liberties are protected.[48]

Several key agencies are tasked with contributing to the success of this strategic objective, especially the Department of Homeland Security (DHS), and several intelligence and law enforcement agencies. Multiple official reports identify the above tasks as essential to homeland defense and protection from terrorist attack.[49] Accomplishments and the agencies involved are identified by NCTC Director Matthew Olsen:

> The government has disrupted terrorist attacks in the United States and abroad. Our intelligence officers have worked diligently to identify and stop terrorist plots before they are executed. And we have investigated and prosecuted individuals who have sought to carry out and support terrorist operations. In addition, we have continued to build an enduring counterterrorism framework—including institutions like NCTC and DHS [Department of Homeland Security]—dedicated to analyzing and sharing terrorism information across the government and to the mission of detecting and preventing terrorist attacks against our citizens and interests around the world. The credit for these successes belongs to the men and women in our military, law enforcement and intelligence communities.[50]

President Obama, in his May 2013 NDU speech, identifies these same accomplishments while also stating that his approach will abide by differing "rule of law" standards than his White House predecessor, "... we strengthened our defenses—hardening targets, tightening transportation security, and giving law enforcement new tools to prevent terror."[51] A generally laudatory report issued September 2011 finds that 10 years after 9/11, of the 15 recommendations made by the 2004 *9/11 Commission Report* directed at protecting against and preparing for terrorist attacks, nine have been fulfilled:

- terrorist travel
- border security
- international cooperation on border security
- transportation security
- improved aviation security
- safeguard privacy of information
- executive branch department to ensure civil liberties/security tradeoff legally enforced
- objective risk assessment determines allocation of homeland security assistance
- private sector preparedness

Seven recommendations required improvement or remain unfulfilled:
- biometric entry-exit
- secure identification
- better passenger explosive screening
- justification of executive privilege
- entitlement to civil liberties
- incident command system adoption
- radio spectrum sharing.[52]

Data on terrorist incidents in the United States, intelligence disruption of terrorist plots, legal actions against terrorist plotters, and official response to the April 15, 2013, Boston marathon terror attack largely also corroborate the considerable successes in pursuit of this strategic objective.[53] It is important to note, finally, these tasks essential to strategic objective #3 are the primary responsibility of the Department of Justice, DHS, (created in 2002; combines 22 existing federal agencies, workforce of 230,000, and budget exceeding $50 billion), the NCTC, and the Office of the Director of National Intelligence (ODNI).[54]

Preventing the Continued Growth of Islamist Terrorism.

Compared with the previous two strategic objectives above, preventing the continued growth of Islamist terrorism has proven the most challenging.[55] Indeed, during the past 4 years, challenges on this front have emerged as a source of official reports, commentary, concern, and perplexity. A seemingly battered and bruised AQ, reeling from 5 years of ramped up drone attacks and 12 years of post-9/11 USG CT policy and national vigilance, has somehow managed to solicit and elicit the participation of hundreds, if not thousands, of persons radicalized by its propaganda and recruited to any number of terrorist plots. Debate at present among CT analysts and policymakers concerns not **whether** new recruits are making themselves available for terrorist acts, but **how** to conceptualize this phenomenon, and **what** strategies are required to combat it.

Official pronouncements of this emergent phenomenon are legion. Let us first consider a few of the more prominent official USG accounts. The Bipartisan Commission charged with evaluating the implementation of the 2004 Commission's recommendations 10 years after 9/11 asserts:

> Although Osama bin Laden is dead, al Qaeda is not; it is a network, not a hierarchy. Over a period of years, al Qaeda has been very adaptive and resilient. . . . Al Qaeda's capabilities to implement large-scale attacks are less formidable than they were ten years ago, but al Qaeda and its affiliates continue to have the intent and reach to kill dozens, or even hundreds, of Americans in a single attack. Al Qaeda has been marked by rapid decentralization. The most significant threats

to American national security come from affiliates of core al Qaeda . . . [al-Awlaki and AQAP; South Asia]; . . . failing or failed states such as Yemen and Somalia. . . . al Qaeda's strategy of 'diversification' — attacks mounted by a wide variety of perpetrators of different national and ethnic backgrounds that cannot easily be 'profiled' as threats. . . . Most troubling, we have seen a pattern of increasing terrorist recruitment of American citizens and residents to act as 'lone wolves'. Today, we know that Americans are playing increasingly prominent roles in al Qaeda's movement. Muslim-American youth are being recruited in Somali communities in Minneapolis and Portland, Oregon, in some respects moving the front lines to the interior of our country. . . . Alarmingly, we have discovered that individuals in the U.S. are engaging in 'self-radicalization'. This process is often influenced by blogs and other online content advocating violent Islamist extremism. While there are methods to monitor some of this activity, it is simply impossible to know the inner thinking of every at-risk person. Thus, self-radicalization poses a serious emerging threat in the U.S.[56]

A similar characterization of this emergent phenomenon is described in the 2011 *National Strategy for Counterterrorism* (NSCT). For example:

[I]n recent years the source of the threat to the United States and its allies has shifted in part toward the periphery — to groups affiliated with but separate from the core group in Pakistan and Afghanistan. This also includes deliberate efforts by al-Qa'ida to inspire individuals within the United States to conduct attacks on their own.[57]

The broadened definition of an "adherent" in this NSCT also evidences this shift: adherent is defined as

[i]ndividuals who have formed collaborative relationships with, act on behalf of, or are otherwise inspired
to take action in furtherance of the goals of al-Qa'ida —
the organization and the ideology — including by engaging in violence regardless of whether such violence is targeted at the United States, its citizens, or its
interests.[58]

A litany of similar warnings is sounded at
various places.

Although its brutal tactics and mass murder of Muslims have undermined its appeal, al-Qa'ida has had
some success in rallying individuals and other militant groups to its cause. Where its ideology does reso-
nate, the United States faces an evolving threat from
groups and individuals that accept al-Qa'ida's agenda
whether through formal alliance, loose affiliation, or
mere inspiration. . . . Adherence to al-Qa'ida's ideology may not require allegiance to al-Qa'ida, the organization. Individuals who sympathize with or actively
support al-Qa'ida may be inspired to violence and can
pose an ongoing threat, even if they have little or no
formal contact with al-Qa'ida. Global communications
and connectivity place al-Qa'ida's calls for violence
and instructions for carrying it out within easy reach
of millions. Precisely because its leadership is under
such pressure in Afghanistan and Pakistan, al-Qa'ida
has increasingly sought to inspire others to commit
attacks in its name. Those who in the past have attempted attacks in the United States have come from
a wide range of backgrounds and origins, including
U.S. citizens and individuals with varying degrees of
overseas connections and affinities.[59]

[We] must retain a focus on addressing the near-term
challenge of preventing those individuals already on
the brink from embracing al-Qa'ida ideology and re-
sorting to violence.[60]

. . . [P]lots directed and planned from overseas are not the only sort of terrorist threat we face. Individuals inspired by but not directly connected to al-Qa'ida have engaged in terrorism in the U.S. Homeland. Others are likely to follow their example, and so we must remain vigilant.[61]

Europe also faces a threat from individuals radicalized by al-Qa'ida ideology to carry out violence despite their lack of formal affiliation with or operational direction from al-Qa'ida or its affiliates.[62]

The 21st century venue for sharing information and ideas is global, and al-Qa'ida, its affiliates and its adherents attempt to leverage the worldwide reach of media and communications systems to their advantage. . . . In the global information environment, al-Qa'ida adherents who promote or attempt to commit violence domestically are influenced by al-Qa'ida ideology and messaging that originates overseas, and those who attempt terror overseas often cite domestic U.S. events or policies. At the same time, people — including those targeted by al-Qa'ida propaganda — live in a local context and are affected by local issues, media, and concerns."[63]

It is clear that al-Qa'ida the organization has been degraded and out of weakness, called on individuals who know the group only through its ideology to carry out violence in its name. . . . And even as the core of al-Qa'ida in Pakistan and Afghanistan continues to be dismantled through systematic CT actions, we have expanded our focus in this Strategy to articulate the specific approaches we must take to counter al-Qa'ida affiliates and adherents on the periphery, be they established affiliated groups in Yemen or Somalia or individual adherents in the Homeland who may be mobilized to violence in al-Qa'ida's name. . . . As some threats have been diminished, others have emerged, and—correspondingly—as some of our approach remain constant, so have others evolved.[64]

NCTC Director Olsen, after having cited great progress along strategic objectives one and three,[65] similarly remarks:[66]

> While these gains are real and enduring, al-Qa'ida, its affiliates and adherents around the world—as well as other terrorist organizations—continue to pose a significant threat to our country. This threat is resilient, adaptive, and persistent. More than a decade after the September 11th attacks, we remain at war with al-Qa'ida, and we face an evolving threat from its affiliates and adherents. . . . Indeed, the threats we face have become more diverse. As al-Qa'ida core leadership struggles to remain relevant, the group has turned to its affiliates and adherents to carry out attacks and to advance its ideology. The group remains committed to striking Western targets, including the United States . . . compel[ling] operational planners to place a greater emphasis on smaller, simpler plots that are easier to carry out . . . Since Bin Laden's death, multiple al-Qa'ida leaders have publicly endorsed the concept of individual acts of violence . . . .

> Homegrown violent extremists (HVEs), including those inspired by al-Qa'ida's ideology, continue to pose a threat to the United States. HVEs inspired by al-Qa'ida are almost certainly entering a period of transition as US-based violent extremists adjust to the deaths and disruption of influential English-language figures who helped al-Qa'ida's ideas resonate with some in the U.S. Now deceased AQAP members Anwar al-Aulaqi and Samir Khan were probably best positioned to create propaganda specifically for an American audience and mobilize HVEs. Their propaganda remains easily accessible online and will likely continue to inspire HVE violence. The growth of online English-

language extremist content during the last three years [2009-2012] has fostered a shared identity — but not necessarily operational collaboration — among HVEs. Plots disrupted during the past year were unrelated operationally, but may demonstrate a common cause rallying independent violent extremists to plot against the US. Lone actors or insular groups pose the most serious HVE threat to the homeland. HVEs could view lone offender attacks as a model for future plots in the United States and overseas. The perceived success of previous lone offender attacks combined with al-Qa'ida and AQAP's propaganda promoting individual acts of terrorism is raising the profile of this tactic"[67]

In recent Congressional testimony, DNI Clapper proposes a nearly identical assessment when he asserts that "[t]errorist threats are in a transition period as the global jihadist movement becomes increasingly decentralized" and comprises the following actors of deepest concern to the USG.[68] Core AQ will continue its targeting of the United States as noted above, but one now must consider the following delineating and disaggregation of the contemporary threat landscape. AQAP's continued attempt to hit the U.S. homeland but also adjust its own techniques, tactics, and procedures in relation to more local objectives; AQ-inspired HVEs which he estimates "will continue to be involved in fewer than 10 domestic plots per year" and will be motivated to engage in violent action by global jihadist propaganda, including English-language material, such as AQAP's *Inspire* magazine; events in the United States or abroad perceived to be threatening to Muslims; the perceived success of other HVE plots, such as the November 2009 attack at Fort Hood, TX, and March 2012 attacks by an AQ-inspired extremist in Toulouse, France; and their own grievances.

In a discussion of the "global jihadist threat overseas" including "affiliates, allies, and sympathizers," Clapper states that despite AQ's complete absence in fomenting the "Arab Spring," it presents "opportunities for established affiliates, aspiring groups, and like-minded individuals to conduct attacks against US interests"; that the Arab Spring will also increase the likelihood of diminished state capacities that will facilitate:

> weakened or diminished counterterrorism capabilities, border control mechanisms, internal security priorities, and other shortcomings in these countries — [that] combined with anti-US grievances or triggering events — will sustain the threats to US interests throughout the region.[69]

The President's 2013 NDU speech makes repeated reference to the evolving threat environment now confronting U.S. CT policy and strategy. Referencing "core AQ" and "regional affiliates" in Africa, Yemen, Somalia, and Iraq in terms identical to NCTC Director Olsen and DNI Clapper, Obama explicitly identifies the rise of home-based and home-grown radicalization and recruitment to terror[70]:

> Finally, we face a real threat from radicalized individuals here in the United States. Whether it's a shooter at a Sikh Temple in Wisconsin; a plane flying into a building in Texas; or the extremists who killed 168 people at the Federal Building in Oklahoma City — America has confronted many forms of violent extremism in our time. Deranged or alienated individuals — often U.S. citizens or legal residents — can do enormous damage, particularly when inspired by larger notions of violent jihad. That pull towards extremism appears to have led to the shooting at Fort Hood, and the bombing of the Boston Marathon. . . .[71]

A recent report[72] to the United Nations (UN) Security Council by a team responsible for reporting on the implementation and success of sanctions pursuant to Resolution 2083 (2012) concerning AQ, associated individuals, and entities similarly finds:

- that the AQ threat continues to diversify, with the evolution of a range of loosely linked affiliates and the rise of autonomously radicalized individuals and cells drawing on AQ's ideology. While the threat posed by AQ as a global terrorist organization has declined, the threat posed by its affiliates and infectious ideas persists.[73]
- Three developments point to the continuing evolution of the threat. First, terrorist propaganda on the Internet continues to grow in sophistication and reach, and is contributing to the problem of self-radicalization. Second, the recent attacks in Boston, London, and Paris point to the persistent challenge of acts of expressive terrorist violence committed by individuals or small groups. Troublingly, these may draw on autonomous attack plans rather than the specific leadership tasking of either AQ or affiliates.[74] Third, the continuing civil war in the Syrian Arab Republic has seen the emergence of a strong AQ in Iraq . . . attracting hundreds of recruits from outside the Syrian Arab Republic.[75]
- AQ and its affiliates have shown themselves to be adept communicators, using marketing and propaganda to cultivate supporters and incite attacks.[76]

Finally, academic analysts Schweitzer and Mendelbaum make several keen observations on AQ's recent prospects, despite being damaged over the past decade by a global anti-terrorist regime. "[T]he leaders of al-Qaeda and its affiliates," they assert, "chose to adopt the Arab Spring in order to turn it into an Islamic Spring." By exploiting toppled regimes, forming opportunistic tactical alliances, wreaking chaos, fomenting ungovernability, taking advantage of security lapses, and streaming in foreign fighters, it may be the case that:

> al-Zawahiri's vision of establishing a caliphate and restoring Islam's lost glory seems imaginary, [however], it is likely that al-Qaeda, by means of its affiliates and perhaps also on its own, will try to renew its efforts to carry out a grand terrorist campaign, as it did in the past, following the withdrawal of the United States and NATO from Afghanistan.[77]

Daily headlines and the increased probabilities associated with terrorist action arising in a less centralized fashion and involving persons more recently recruited to a so-called jihadist path typify larger swaths of contemporary life. It is one thing to be treated to high level reports, analyses, policies, pronouncements, and findings, and another to assemble the raw data centering on individual persons whose acts or potential acts lead them to find the very publicity they seek.

We earlier listed some of Awlaki's most prominent terrorist recruits — Major Nidal Malik Hassan, Dzohar and Tamerlan Tsarnaev, Zachary Adam Chesser, Umar Farouk Abdulmutallab, Shahzad Faisal, and Carlos Leon Bledsoe. Let us now consider the briefest sampling of others whose names have graced headlines in recent years:

- Bangladeshi Quazi Mohammed Rezwanul Ahsan Nafis, 21, arrested in a sting operation involving a fake 1,000-pound VIED bomb.[78]
- Jose Pimentel, a 27 year-old Muslim convert of Hispanic origin; a follower of Awlaki, constructed the bombs based on *Inspire's* "Make a Bomb in the Kitchen of Your Mom."[79]
- Naser Abdo, 21, a professed conscientious objector based on his Muslim beliefs:

> found in a motel room three miles from Fort Hood's main gate with a handgun, an article titled "Make a Bomb in the Kitchen of Your Mom" from AQAP's English-language *Inspire* magazine and the ingredients for an explosive device, including gunpowder, shrapnel, and pressure cookers. . . . Abdo told investigators he planned to construct two bombs in his motel room using gunpowder and shrapnel packed into pressure cookers and then detonate the explosives at a restaurant frequented by soldiers. . . . On his way out of the courtroom he yelled "Iraq 2006!" and the name of Abeer Qassim al-Janabi, a 14-year-old Iraqi girl who was raped that year before she and her family were killed. Five current or former soldiers went to prison, one for a life term, for their roles in that attack. He also shouted the name of Hasan, an Army major and psychiatrist charged with killing 13 people at Fort Hood.[80]

- Mohammed Mahmood Alessa, 20 (born in the United States and of Palestinian descent), and Carlos Eduardo Almonte, 26 (naturalized citizen born in Dominican Republic), arrested before boarding separate flights for Egypt and then to Somalia, June 5, 2010, for planning an assassination to outdo Major Nidal Malik Hassan. "He's not better than me. I'll do twice what he did," Alessa allegedly said in undercover recordings by New York Police Department undercover officers.[81]

- Rezwan Ferdaus, 27, studied physics at Northeastern University in Boston, his family resident in Ashland, MA, an upscale suburb west of Boston, "admitted to planning to blow up the Pentagon and the United States Capitol using remote-controlled planes laden with explosives"; sentenced to 17 years in prison.[82]
- Adel Daoud, an 18-year-old suburban Chicago man arrested for attempting to detonate what he thought was a car bomb outside a Chicago bar. . . . [He] had been under surveillance for months, and in multiple conversations with agents expressed a desire to kill on a mass scale as revenge for what he believed was the persecution of Muslims by the United States.[83]
- Walli Mujahidh, 34, was one of two men who planned to storm the Military Entrance Processing Station south of downtown Seattle with machine guns and grenades in retaliation for U.S. military actions in Afghanistan. Enlistees are screened and processed at the station. The other conspirator Abu Khalid Abdul-Latif, also known as Joseph Anthony Davis, was sentenced to 18 years in prison last month. The pair, both U.S. citizens, were arrested in June 2011 and pleaded guilty of the attempted murder of officers and agents of the United States and conspiracy to use weapons of mass destruction. Grenades are treated as weapons of mass destruction under U.S. federal law.[84]

- Gufran Ahmed Kauser Mohammed, a 30-year-old naturalized U.S. citizen born in India, and Mohamed Hussein Said, a 25-year-old Kenyan, were "accused of having used Western Union to wire a total of $96,000 to an al Qaeda affiliate, al-Nusra Front . . . and al Shabaab" in Somalia. The money was to help Said in getting fighters out of Africa and into Syria. The men have also been accused of recruiting or trying to recruit individuals overseas to join rebels linked to al-Qaeda.[85]

Residents of various European countries also awaken to similar headlines. Consider for example:
- Seven suspects between 22 and 32 years of age, all described as British residents, arrested in an anti-terror operation.[86]
- Three Muslim immigrants to Norway were arrested for a terrorist plot; a Uighur from China, an Iraqi Kurd, and an Uzbek, had ties to operatives of AQ in the tribal areas of Pakistan, all members of the Turkistan Islamic Party, a Uighur separatist group based largely in the lawless Pakistani tribal area of Waziristan.[87]
- Three men, born in Britain of Pakistani origin, were found guilty of the 2006 conspiracy to attack seven transatlantic airliners bound for the United States and Canada with liquid bombs. In all, 10 men faced charges in the case that involved three separate criminal trials; all but two were convicted. . . . Scotland Yard, describing its effort as the most elaborate terrorism investigation it has ever mounted, said the costs of the police operations alone amounted to nearly $40 million. The case involved the deployment of 29

separate surveillance teams during the months the plotters were under observation and was said to have been the most costly investigation in the force's history. . . . The bombs the plotters prepared for the attacks, consisting of liquid explosive inserted by syringes into plastic soft-drink bottles, led to tight new restrictions on the liquids and creams passengers can take onto flights. . . . Prosecutors at the trials said the plot, if successful, would have caused deaths on a scale comparable to the 9/11 attacks, and most of the potential toll of 1,500 to 2,000 victims were likely to have been Americans. . .[88]

- Taimor Abdulwahab al-Abdaly, 28, a disaffected Iraqi Swede, detonated two bombs, killing only himself. A Swedish citizen, he had been living in Britain for the past 10 years.[89]
- Raed Jaser, 35, born in the United Arab Emirates (UAE) to Palestinian parents but not a UAE citizen, was living in Toronto at the time of his arrest, and Tunisian-born, Chiheb Esseghaier, 30, both arrested in plot to derail a Via passenger train running between New York City and Montreal. Charged with conspiring to carry out an attack and murder people in association with a terrorist group, they could face life in prison if convicted. . . . A few weeks after Esseghaier and Jaser were arrested, FBI officials arrested a Tunisian man in New York who they said was linked to the Via rail terror plot. Ahmed Abassi was charged with trying to stay in the United States illegally to build a cell for international acts of terror. Prosecutors said Abassi had radicalized Esseghaier. The indictment charges Abassi with two counts of lying

on applications for a green card and work visa. Each count carries a maximum term of 25 years in prison upon conviction.[90]

- Zahid Iqba, Mohammaed Sharfaraz Ahmed, Umar Arshad, and Syed Farhan Hussain, between 22 and 31 years of age, were jailed in Britain on Thursday for discussing terrorist attacks, including plans to blow up an army reserve center using a bomb-laden toy car. They downloaded files containing instructions for the attack, bought survival equipment and collected money for terrorist purposes. The men were recorded discussing sending a remote-controlled toy car carrying a homemade bomb under the gates of an army reservist center and speaking of using instructions in an AQ manual to make an improvised explosive device. Iqbal and Ahmed were jailed for 16 years and 3 months, while Arshad received a sentence of 6 years and 9 months. Hussain was jailed for 5 years and 3 months.[91]

- Irfan Naseer, Irfan Khalid, and Ashik Ali planned to detonate up to eight rucksack bombs in a suicide attack or set off timber bombs in crowded areas. . . . Prosecutor Altman said the plot was "on a scale potentially greater" than the July 7, 2005, bombings that killed 52 people on London's underground train and bus networks and that "the defendants were inspired to commit terrorism by the anti-Western sermons of U.S.-born radical cleric Anwar al-Awlaki."[92]

- Michael Adebolajo, 28, born in Britain to a Christian family that moved to Britain from Nigeria, who converted to Islam at approximately age 16, after the 9/11 attacks, and Michael Adebowale, 22 born in Nigeria and immigrated to Britain as a child, brutally murdered Lee Rigby, aged 25, an infantryman in the Royal Fusiliers, and drummer who performed ceremonial guard duties at Buckingham Palace, while Rigby was walking near a military barracks in south London. He was first rammed by a car and then hacked to death by these two knife-wielding — meat cleaver and kitchen-knife — assailants, one of the men shouted *"Allahu Akbar,"* or "God is great," as the attack proceeded. A man who appeared to be in his 20s or early 30s held a cleaver in one of his bloodied hands. He offered what seemed to be a political message before the police arrived. "I apologize that women had to see this today, but in our lands women have to see the same thing," he said. "You people will never be safe. Remove your governments! They don't care about you." He then referred to what appeared to be a motive for the attack, saying it was carried out, "Because of what's going on in our own countries." Britain has suffered more than any other country in Northern Europe from Islamic terrorist plots in recent years, and it has worked assiduously to prevent more. Security officials have said that at any given time they are tracking hundreds of young men in extremist networks.[93]

The phenomenon of radicalization and recruitment to various emergent non-U.S. conflict zones before and after the Arab Spring is another noteworthy development.[94] Again, a nonrandom sample of various recent news accounts may be perused in support.[95]

MESSAGE RESONANCE AND U.S. CREDIBILITY IN THE MUSLIM WORLD: USG DEEDS, ACTIONS, AND POLICIES AS COMMUNICATION

A voluminous literature exists analyzing, evaluating, and proposing policies to counter (self-) radicalization and (self-) recruitment to AQ-based, affiliated, associated, or inspired terrorist attacks. A panoply of psychological and sociological variables is proposed as predictors of terrorist actions. These include: being male, aged 16-44, occupationally marginalized, religiously intolerant or a new religious convert, exhibiting an unstable or crisis-prone social identity, personally maladaptive, and possessing a lack of psychosocial resilience.[96] However, as Sageman points out, though these states and traits are undoubtedly significant and at least partially descriptive of persons who engage in terrorist acts,[97] tens or hundreds of millions of persons worldwide exhibit these same states and traits who do **not** engage in terrorist behaviors. More problematic for purely compensatory theories of terrorist behavior, the vast majority does not exhibit any abnormal psychological or psychosocial traits, and many lead relatively successful lives, both materially and relationally.

Moreover, psychologically normal affective bases underpinning terrorist motivation — anger, moral indignation, moral outrage, or at its outermost limit, categorical hate — sufficiently explain why many terrorist recruits self-deploy as human bombs and killers. Revenge and retribution for perceived wrongs committed against Muslims is cited as justification, again and again, exceeding by a huge factor excuses or justifications made in the name of Islam or shari'a, let alone the jurisprudence governing the fighting of jihad (*fiqh al-jihad*.⁹⁸ Rather, it is because these persons perceive that the West generally and the United States in particular is **at war** with Islam — oppressing, aggressing, humiliating, murdering, and exploiting Muslims — that terrorist acts are, in their minds, morally justified. Finally, this empathy and moral indignation are considerably enabled by both a real or vicarious identification as "fictive kin" of the worldwide Islamic umma or faith community, and an actual kinship among diasporic populations.⁹⁹

If one excepts abnormal psychological traits among select lone-wolf terrorists, then countering radicalization and recruitment to AQ terrorism requires that one abandon the hunt for the "terrorist mind" and take up the task of countering the (mis-) perception that the United States is an aggressive, oppressive, and exploitative power truly **at war** with and **inexorably hostile** to Islam. This task entails engaging three key psychological variables — perception (cognition), affect (emotions), and behavior (volition) — causally related in the following manner: Changing perception from one of oppression, to one of fairness and fair dealing ordinarily diminishes one's sense of moral indignation and outrage. This diminished moral outrage ordinarily eliminates the desire to seek retributive justice, and in extreme cases, violent revenge. Finally, the dissolution of a desire for violent revenge against one or one's (real or fictive) kinsman's perceived oppressors greatly reduces the likelihood one will be self-recruited to engage in terrorist acts.¹⁰⁰

If the United States **is** at war with Islam and Muslims worldwide, it stands to reason that one **must** attack and confront the American foe. It would not be an act of cowardice, but one of courage, to do so. It would involve sacrificing possibly one's life, estate, and friends and family; for some, exiting a life of relative security, privilege, and opportunity. But the defense of the defenseless against a perceived predatory power requires that one leave this life behind, and that after this life, Allah's favor will more than make up for the fears, tears, and disrupted lives that this sacrificial death entails. These affective variables — revenge, moral outrage, retribution, payback, defense of one's religion, and defense of one's people — I believe, must be fully understood and combated at the level they require.[101]

* * * * *

In the remainder of this monograph, a distinct method is proposed for countering the perception that the United States is at war with Islam, the moral outrage it inspires, and the terrorist response it too often enjoins. I shall call this method "a War of Deeds" or "counterpropaganda of the deed." The latter phrase, analytically compelling and a time-honored military art, may nevertheless be tainted by the negative attributes associated with the term "propaganda." The former War of Deeds avoids the stigma of "propaganda" and offers the twin benefit of contrast to a "war of ideas" approach, the problems of which will be identified at appropriate points. Further, by emphasizing deeds, actions, and USG policies, rather than words, intentions, and promises, we shift the primary battleground to one of countering enemy propaganda with facts and evidence that I believe can, if deftly crafted in a systematic, sustained campaign, eviscerate AQ's fabrications and lies. This proposed War of Deeds is offered as a distinct, realistic, and credible approach for neutralizing, combating, and ultimately obliterating the affective outrage propelling recruits to place their lives at the service of AQ's terrorist modus operandi. It is to be fought on two fronts, "changing deeds" and "challenging deeds."

Changing deeds, the first front, enhances the resonance of the USG message in the Arab and Muslim world through actively fostering policies that reinforce, amplify, and increase the probable success of the second front—challenging AQ's disinformation, fabrications, lies, and distortions.

Changing deeds requires that the USG honestly examine the actual impact of U.S. foreign and military policy in the greater Muslim world. It is imperative that the USG make the case in deeds, actions, and official policies, not intentions or promises, that the United States is **not at war** with Islam or Muslims, and is indeed a formidable power whose interests, values, and ultimate objectives are **not inimical** to Islam and the Islamic faith, the Islamic Call and Muslim interests. It is not perfection, but the proven absence of enmity or active pursuit of policies, deeds, or actions designed to denude and destroy Islam, or predatory waging of war against a weak and defenseless umma, that must be proved.

Challenging deeds, the second front, requires that the USG successfully refute AQ's propaganda, disinformation, fabrications, and distortions regarding the practical consequences of U.S. deeds, policies, and actions, **and** of AQ's own, in the Muslim world.

These two interrelated tasks have a common objective: persuasively proving in deeds, actions, policies, and actual behaviors that the USG is **not** at war with Muslims and Islam. That this must be proven and not taken for granted; that this not be seen as an exercise akin to combating holocaust denial or the 9/11 "truthers" is essential. It is not essential that the United States be innocent of superpower motives, actions, intentions, or behaviors; nor that, there is no national dirty laundry, past or present, to discuss. What is essential is that we prove that these actions do not signify any type of ongoing, systematic enmity directed at Islam, Muslims, or the Arab World in particular. We must prove this even though USG actions may on occasion signify other potentially unsavory interests and alliances, as well as many potentially and actually beneficent means and ends. In short, what must be proved, through the evidence of deeds and not intentions, promises, or attempts at spin, is that the United States is not now and has never been at war with Islam and does not actively desire nor require its negation. Furthermore, the USG must prove it is innocent of all charges of intentionally targeting, harming, or fostering aggression against or oppression of Muslims on account of faith or works.

CHANGING DEEDS AND ENHANCING MESSAGE RESONANCE

Changing deeds is key to enhancing message resonance and is the necessary first front in a sustained campaign to counter radicalization and recruitment to AQ-inspired terrorism. This premise rests on three propositions. First, there is widespread recognition among officials charged with enhancing U.S. credibility, that deeds, actions, and policies **are** persuasive communication. As we will soon see, official attempts to obscure this simple fact through public diplomacy or strategic communication are doomed to fail. Second, considerable literature comprised of official USG policies and reports from government oversight bodies, academics, and think tanks concludes that opposition to American foreign and military policies, and **not** to Americans or American values per se, are key drivers of anti-American animus and the proximate cause for declining U.S. credibility and standing in the Arab and Muslim world. Third, despite anti-American animus motivated by opposition to U.S. foreign and military policies, however, no objective evidence exists of any officially-sanctioned USG "Crusader" war being waged against Islam as a religious faith, or Muslim adherents to that faith. Let us examine these in turn.

The Limits of Public Diplomacy and Strategic Communication: Or, the "Lipstick on Pigs" Problem.[102]

The *Information Operations Primer* defines "Strategic Communication" as "the orchestration of actions, words, and images to achieve cognitive effects in support of policy and military objectives."[103] Though all communicative elements are important, U.S. Army information operations specialists most especially view actions to be as effective and successful strategic communication. Actions "speak for themselves" and signify the assurance of intentions and values far more than promises and platitudes. Though primarily written with specific military operations in mind, the following assertion can easily be generalized to human actions:

> [S]enior officials point out that strategic communication is '80% actions, and 20% words.' Specifically, how military operations are conducted affects the information environment by impacting perceptions, attitudes and beliefs . . . [and] . . . how military operations are

conducted or policy is implemented is also a key component of strategic communication, since actions send very loud and clear messages.[104]

The primacy of actions is also evident in a criticism of the concept "strategic communications" by retired admiral Michael Mullen, former chairman of Joint Chiefs of Staff. In opposition to a "marketing model of countering Taliban propaganda being promoted by the Rendon Group," Mullen reportedly refuses to even use the phrase strategic communication and insists simply on providing "information and context about military operations." He declares:

> I really do not like the term at all. It confuses people. . . . It means all things to all people. It's way overused and overrated. I literally try never to use the term. *We communicate as much if not more by our actions.* I have become particularly concerned at a time that resources are so precious. It has become a thing unto itself. It is taking resources from the fight. I don't have time for it. (emphasis added).[105]

Actions are deemed key to the more general concept of information operations as well. The purpose of information operations is:

> . . . to influence the behavior of target decision-makers while simultaneously defending friendly decision-makers from being influenced by an adversary's use of information. This is no different from the exercise of the other forms of national power. In this instance the means is information, but the resulting outcome is the same.[106]

The key role of actions among forms of influence, however, is well noted:

> [P]ersonal interactions are perhaps the most important means a target audience can be influenced. In the context of persuasive influence, these interactions can range from compulsion and coercion on one end of the spectrum to cooperation and collaboration on the other. . . . Regardless of how a message is transmitted, the credibility of our messages and messengers is key to the effectiveness of our influence efforts. *We must recognize that we lose credibility when the implied messages of our actions do not match the messages of our covert communications.* If these messages are not coordinated during the IO planning process, our credibility and effectiveness suffer (emphasis added).[107]

Other agencies also recognize the role of deeds in general, as well as the vital role of deeds in diagnosing and diminishing the present U.S. credibility gap in the Arab and Muslim world. However, unlike the matter-of-fact role ascribed to actions above, this explicit recognition of the importance of deeds frequently gets dialed down and packaged in strategies far less bold than demanded. Minimizing the importance of deeds shows a failure of imagination or an unwillingness to fully consider the implications of one's premises at best. At worst, charges of inconsistency, incoherence or even duplicity may be leveled. Some examples of this behavior and its results follow.

Let us first consider one of the earliest examples of this schizoid character. It actually calls for putting "lipstick on a pig" in order to make what are undesirable policies appear something other than they are. Just over a month after 9/11, Richard Holbrooke, then-ambassador to the UN, issued one of the earliest alarms to policymakers and the public of our apparently inexplicable failure to counter what then appeared to be the unstoppable juggernaut of Osama bin Laden's propaganda. Consider the following assertion:

> Call it public diplomacy, or public affairs, or psycho-
> logical warfare, or—if you really want to be blunt—
> propaganda. But whatever it is called, defining what
> this war is really about in the minds of 1 billion Mus-
> lims in the world will be of decisive and historic im-
> portance. Yet every expert in Islam, every analyst of
> what is happening in the Muslim world, agrees that
> Osama bin Laden has gained the initial advantage in
> this struggle by arguing that this is a war against Is-
> lam, rather than, as President Bush correctly says, a
> war against terrorism. At first glance, this seems in-
> credible: How could a mass murderer who publicly
> praised the terrorists of Sept. 11 be winning the hearts
> and minds of anyone? How can a man in a cave out
> communicate the world's leading communications
> society?[108]

To what, then, does Holbrooke attribute this U.S. failure in public diplomacy and strategic communication? "Part of Bin Laden's success lies in his shrewd mix of modern media technologies and medieval symbols," Holbrooke declares, ". . . [a]nother factor is his exploitation of the seething resentment of Arabs toward U.S. support for Israel." Remarkably, Holbrooke then declares each of these elements as "largely outside our control."[109]

Bin Laden's message is out of our control because he "controls his own message," and as for the second, Holbrooke asserts, "we cannot reward terrorism by reducing our support for Israel." But one might ask at this point, isn't it crucial, at the very least, to forthrightly recognize that perceptions of the United States as backer and facilitator of a continuing occupation and humiliation of Palestinian aspirations underpin anti-American animus, and not a hatred of America or Americans, let alone American values? In fact, could not the case be made here that it is precisely the unwillingness to extend these cherished American values of liberty, self-determination, and social justice to the case of the Israel-Palestinian confrontation, or continuing support for repressive autocratic governments—one that profoundly undermines credibility throughout the Arab and Muslim world, as well as many other quarters—that is the elephant in the room? Or, to conclude that it is American hypocrisy, not American ideals and values that underpins the U.S. credibility problem and facilitates resonance of Osama bin Laden's terrorist propaganda?[110]

Instead, Holbrooke offers an unconvincing or, at worst, an incoherent retort. His first move is to cast USG policy against AQ as an ideological war, a so-called "battle of ideas," rather than one based in policies, actions, and deeds. His second tack is to recognize the importance of actions, but in terms that belie the logic of his own admission that a "seething resentment" in the Arab Muslim world must be addressed. Let us consider each in turn.

> What should concern us most urgently are the apparent failure of our own message and the inadequacy of our messengers. If we fail to convince Muslims that this is not a war against Islam but a war against terrorism, if bin Laden succeeds in defining the struggle in his own terms, then he will have succeeded in his goal—even if, as I confidently believe will be the case, he is tracked down and ultimately eliminated. . . . *The battle of ideas therefore is as important as any other aspect of the struggle we are now engaged in*. It must be won. To fix this problem we must address both the message and the messengers (emphasis added).[111]

While important steps, such as "visiting the Islamic Center in DC" and "meetings with leading Muslims and Arab Americans," were immediately taken in the aftermath of September 11, 2001 (9/11), Holbrooke stated afterwards that things have "gone downhill." He believes the missed opportunities that could have prevented this about-face involve the following: failure to open a dialogue with "key Muslim intellectuals" over an errant and murderous misuse of the *Qur'an*, failure to publicize the fact that hundreds of Muslims were also murdered in the terrorist attack on the 9/11, the failure to prove to Muslim women that they would be sent back to a stone age should Bin Laden triumph, and finally, the failure "to find credible Arabic-speaking Muslims to speak the truth about bin Laden."

It is undoubtedly true that leveraging the jurisprudence of lawful jihad, identifying the terrorist violations of that law, and specifying the major sins committed is an important tactic, one that the present writer advocates.[112] However, it is insufficient since only a sliver of potential recruits is apprised of this jurisprudence, and likely bound to it. Also, what does Holbrooke mean by "the truth of Bin Laden"? Who are these "credible Arab-speaking Muslims" who shall speak such a "truth"? For Holbrooke, it is simply inexplicable why the United States could or should be losing this propaganda war: certainly there is **someone** who can say **something** that can undermine the legitimacy of this man who speaks from a cave! Missing here, is any discussion of actions, deeds, and USG policies examined from the point of view of those who may see themselves as potential victims and seek to become agents seeking retribution, even if the method of terror amounts to a morally reprehensible and murderous tactic. But Holbrooke believes, it seems, to even **raise** the question of policy is to "reward terrorism."

Holbrooke concludes his clarion call by identifying the "messengers" required to arrest the decline in, rectify, and fortify U.S. credibility. Actually, the only discussion of messengers he offers had already occurred when Holbrooke invoked "credible Arab-speaking Muslims," as possible ambassadors who will speak to the purity of America's intentions and ideals. He deems these possible ambassadors as "key Muslim intellectuals," or "leading Muslims and Arab Americans." Here, he actually discusses the media required, and more specifically, the agencies required, to mobilize to confront the bin Laden virus. What he suggests is the need for a full-blown national propaganda effort along the lines of World War II and the Cold War.

> A similar special office is essential now. It must be run from the White House, the only place in Washington that can coordinate—by which I mean direct—public affairs activities of State, Defense, Justice, CIA, AID and others toward the Muslim world. More resources will be required; special broadcasting systems dedicated to this cause must be created, not for Afghanistan, but for the entire Muslim world, including Muslims in non-Arab countries such as India and China, and for that matter, Western Europe, where the terror networks are deeply embedded. . . . This must be a sustained effort separate from, but closely allied to, the war on terrorism. In fact, it will last longer than the war itself and would, if successful, have other benefits. . . . We cannot afford to lose; and if we do, a permanent struggle will lead to a permanent crisis— just what bin Laden and his supporters want.[113]

Holbrooke's opinion editorial, penned just 1 month after the 9/11 attacks, presumes that a "battle of ideas" must be fought contrasting an un-Islamic, murderous, diabolical bin Laden seeking the enslavement of Muslim women and the resurrection of a medieval caliphate, with America's true values, virtues, and ideals. "If only they *truly* knew what we truly stand for!" he seems to declare. "If only we could tell the true story of our commitment to human rights, democracy, social justice, and liberty for all! How can a man in a cave out communicate the world's leading communications society?" he asked.[114]

Could he, with deep reflection, have answered that it is not about communicating with high-sounding words or wrapping oneself in glorious ideals. Instead, it is about what we do, not about what we say about what we do. It is about how deeds, policies, and actions *communicate*. It is about the experiences of those who live with the consequences of these policies. It is, in short, very much about the perception of virtually unconditional support for Israel's continuing occupation; of the politics of oil reserves; and the autocrats and monarchs of the Gulf. It is about USG policy and moral outrage. It is about credibility, in fact and in deed, not about the failure of the world's greatest superpower to discover the philosopher's stone revealing the secret message, messengers, and media, required to refute bin Laden. It is the "lipstick on pigs problem," in other words. It is not about ideas, or a "battle of ideas"; it is about deeds, and a War of Deeds.

Approximately 3 years after 9/11 and the inauguration of the Global War on Terror (GWOT), 1 year after the U.S. overthrow of Saddam Hussein and military occupation of Iraq, and 4 years into the second Palestinian intifada, another promising yet highly compromised beginning is in evidence in an early official effort to diagnose what appeared to be an abject failure of U.S. public diplomacy and strategic communication.[115] A careful reading reveals a surprisingly candid analysis of how U.S. policies contribute to this collapse in U.S. credibility.[116] It is a prescient analysis of the rise and power of nonviolent political Islamists, and yet, like Holbrooke, its response is paltry and targets a narrow band of cherry-picked pro-Western secular elites. This response never once considers revisiting U.S. policy priorities to see how they might affect those vast majorities whose opinions are registered in plummeting opinion polls.[117] Let us briefly consider this scathing review of U.S. policies, clear recognition of an ascendant nonviolent political Islam, and impoverished suggested remedies.

By late-2003, virtually every major opinion poll throughout the Arab and Muslim world was registering its lowest ever favorable ratings of the United States. Without question, U.S. credibility was in free fall.[118] The predominant finding of this report is unequivocal:

> Muslims do not 'hate our freedom,' but rather, they hate our policies. The overwhelming majority [in opinion polls] voice their objections to what they see as one-sided support in favor or Israel and against Palestinian rights, and the long-standing, even increasing support for what Muslims collectively see as tyrannies, most notably in Egypt, Saudi Arabia, Jordan, Pakistan, and the Gulf states. . . . Thus the critical problem in American public diplomacy directed toward the Muslim World is not one of 'dissemination of information,' or even one of crafting and delivering the 'right' message. Rather, it is a fundamental problem of credibility. . . .[119]

In another remarkably frank admission, the study authors assert:

> The United States finds itself in the strategically awkward — and potentially dangerous — situation of being the longstanding prop and alliance partner of these authoritarian regimes. Without the U.S. these regimes would not survive. Thus the U.S. has strongly taken sides in a desperate struggle that is both broadly cast for all Muslims *and* country-specific. This is the larger strategic context, and it is acutely uncomfortable: U.S. policies and actions are increasingly seen by the overwhelming majority of Muslims as a threat to the survival of Islam itself.[120]

The report also betrays a very clear-headed analysis of Islamism distinguishing violent revolutionary Islamism from nonviolent reformist Islamisms, each with a similar short-term strategic objective:

> If there is one overarching goal they [Islamists] share, it is the overthrow of what Islamists call the 'apostate' regimes: the tyrannies of Egypt, Saudi Arabia, Pakistan, Jordan, and the Gulf states. They are the main target of the broader Islamist movement, as well as the actual fighter groups.[121]

A prescient analysis is offered of the role that these reformists are likely to play and their closer proximity to the aspirations and approved methods for achieving them supported by an even larger majority.

> [I]t is even more interesting to track the relative weight of the non-Jihadi Islamists, also called "moderate' or "New Islamists,' because their professed vision of Islamic Restoration is non-violent, tolerant, and relatively pluralistic. It can be argued that the New Islamists are in fact the true center of gravity in the Muslim

World today, in that they have the most authority to make change, and draw on the highest levels of sympathy form less-active, but receptive and supportive Arab majorities. In this construct the Jihadis are seen as perhaps necessary to make change begin and thus become eventually inevitable, but the radicals do not appeal to the majority of Muslims in terms of practical change if and when the old regimes finally collapse.[122]

One would expect such candid analysis of the U.S. strategic predicament in the Muslim world could and should lead to a broader debate over policies, priorities, the consequences experienced by the vast masses and the Islamist currents circulating among those masses. Instead, we are treated to the following strategic recommendation. On the one hand, a "revolutionary" strategy requiring the USG should massively inflate the resources dedicated to U.S. communication efforts, including huge expansion in budgets, positions, authority, and a centralized executive-level focus.[123] On the other hand, we should exclusively target and selectively build-up U.S.-friendly agents.

The U.S. Government should target those who support, or are likely to support, our views based on their own culture, traditions and attitudes about such things as personal control, choice and change. Private sector best practices define this as the 'hard support' and 'soft support' in a marketplace and they are not only the likeliest to move in the U.S. Government's direction, but they're also the likeliest to move others. Both their behavior and viral communications form the most powerful and credible medium for attitudinal change. Specifically, for example, we believe the most 'movable' targets will be the so-called secularists of the Muslim world: Business people, scientists, non-religious educators, politicians or public administrators, musicians, artists, poets, writers, journalists, actors and their audiences and admirers.[124]

The report suggests "state of the art practices" derived from advertising, marketing, and political campaigns to accomplish these goals, while assiduously avoiding **any** further discussion of those policies it correctly ascertained were the most significant impediments to U.S. credibility. Nothing is said regarding the grave strategic predicament facing the United States as the final backer and guarantor of regimes deemed tyrannical, autocratic, and undemocratic, or as a state opposed to the legitimate aspirations of Palestinians. Instead this report insists that a secular elite will assist us in lipstick sales, all along knowing and actually having described in this Report the pigs for which it is destined.

Several USG documents or high-level analyses throughout the decade exhibit similar failures to boldly rethink U.S. policies and their relation to U.S. credibility in the Arab and Muslim world. In the June 2007 *U.S. National Strategy for Public Diplomacy and Strategic Communication* issued by the Under Secretary for Public Diplomacy and Public Affairs,[125] we learn of the importance of the diplomacy of deeds,[126] the importance of counterpropaganda, the necessity of countering AQ disinformation and propaganda in cyberspace through further expanding the mission of the existing State Department Digital Outreach Team (DOT), and the necessity for a new Counterterrorist Communications Center.[127] Yet, this diplomacy of deeds is reduced to displays of U.S. humanitarianism during times of disaster, famine, or poverty relief, which, in itself, is insufficient for quelling a deeper animus rooted in our chosen friends, strategic partners, and allies in the region.

Unlike the unvarnished 2004 Defense Science Board discussion of the deeper policy roots of the U.S. decline in credibility, this report obliterates this dimension entirely. Again, unlike the 2004 report, it presumes a "Good Muslim/Bad Muslim dichotomy" which entirely fails to understand the fissures that exist within Islam over AQ's means and ends. Like the 2004 report, however, it entirely neglects potential Islamist and conservative allies and reduces the choices to **either** "mainstream" voices that espouse and embrace secular liberal democracy, **or** AQ presented as a caricatured death cult. AQ is presented without sufficient understanding of the broader phenomenon of Sunni militancy, and the potential of its reformist variants as a form of political Islam not necessarily inimical to U.S. core values and vital interests in the region.[128] There is not a single mention of Israel-Palestine, oil, or autocracy. Offering a compelling list of messaging themes, and correctly defending the necessity of systematic counterpropaganda and leveraging AQ's violations of the shari'a and commission of major sins, one easily concludes that genuine grievances are likely to be assuaged by words, and symbolic humanitarian gestures.

A second Defense Science Task Force report on strategic communication issued in 2008 is a queer creature, combining elements of its 2004 incisiveness with what appears to be a continuing flight from its implications.[129] A promising beginning is made when it states:

> [W]e have changed our thinking in important ways. This report reflects our heightened appreciation that success in strategic communication depends on . . . deep comprehension of the identities, attitudes, cultures, interests, and motives of others . . . awareness

by leaders and practitioners that **what we do** matters more than **what we say**. (p. x; emphasis in original).

So what shall our responses be to the documented rise throughout the decade of anti-Americanism?[130] The Report's authors provide global survey data indicating extremely negative attitudes toward the U.S. occupation of Iraq, increasing support among Muslim and Arab societies for use of suicide attacks in Iraq and especially in the Palestinian territories. One is then treated to the following underwhelming correlations: between tsunami relief in Indonesia and improved attitudes toward Americans, but **not** American policies; and, an even weaker correlation between U.S. earthquake relief in Pakistan, and Pakistani attitudes toward Americans or American policies. It is not just that the correlations are weak, but that perceptions of U.S. policies remain unchanged, despite gratitude and improved attitudes toward the American public. Symbolic and life-saving humanitarian gestures **as** communication is certainly welcome, and necessary. But the same persons who welcome such assistance do not, as a result, abandon deep and abiding attachments and commitments to their sisters and brothers perceived to be suffering under varying forms of occupation, oppression, and tyranny.

In a section entitled "Implications for Strategic Communication," another promising beginning is made when the authors assert: "Disseminating information and 'getting the message right' are not top priorities. Trust, credibility, actions, legitimacy, and reputations are critical to success."[131] Rather than identify concretely what policies and actions may lead to trust, credibility, actions, legitimacy, and reputations however, the report then strangely references the need for messaging and various types of messengers.

Many federal, state, and local nongovernmental, corporate, and individual enterprises originating in the United States are involved in strategic communication with foreign audiences. While there is no single enterprise performing the role of program leader, each program relies on many essential contributions from beyond the domain of its central team to accomplish its goals.

In the above statement, there is not a single mention of any actions, deeds, or policies **whatsoever**. In a final flourish of suggested actions, in a section entitled "Personal Interactions as Compelling Messages," the following are suggested as vital to improving U.S. credibility throughout the Muslim and Arabic world: the Fulbright scholarship program, foreign student exchange programs, U.S. Agency for International Development (USAID) programs, the Peace Corps, lifesaving outreach, and military to military exchanges.[132]

It is hard to understand why "American Foreign and Military Policy in the Arab and Muslim World" **are not** included as having compelling messages. It is as if we cannot understand how someone can **like you**, but still not like **what you are doing or have done**; that one cannot believe that others really do not like how we treat (or they **perceive** how we treat) members of their brethren, despite the fact that, as a people and idea, America is viewed sympathetically. What we do, not who we are—**not** how nice, how generous, how good-hearted, how well-intentioned, how lofty our ideals and commitments to actualizing human potentials; our actions, deeds, and policies—is what is most troublesome and unenviable to these souls.

After a decade's struggle to conceptualize and execute a successful public diplomacy and strategic communication, Congress, via The Duncan Hunter National Defense Authorization Act of Fiscal 2009, required that the President submit "a comprehensive interagency strategy for public diplomacy and strategic communication." Between 2010-12, the President's initial proposal, a Government Accountability Office (GAO) report on that proposal, and an updated presidential proposal, were published.[133] A decade's debate and trial-and-error had further refined the strategic communications conceptual landscape; continued to identify the critical importance of policies, actions, and deeds; though yet again, one is left to feel that the proposed remedies fall far short of those required to refute, counter, and decimate AQ's propaganda.

The objective of strategic communication is clear: "sustaining global legitimacy and supporting our policy aims."[134] How shall this be done? Two distinct methods are advocated: more carefully aligning what we say and what we do (words and deeds); and being deliberate and engaged with the audiences we seek to influence.[135] These two components comprise the very definition of strategic communication:

> (a) the **synchronization of words and deeds** and how they will be perceived by selected audiences, as well as (b) programs and activities **deliberately aimed at communicating and engaging** with intended audiences, including those implemented by public affairs, public diplomacy, and information operations professionals (emphases added).[136]

As conceived then, the problem of strategic communication is primarily one of failed execution, or flawed organization and implementation — a failure to synchronize, a failure to deliberately engage — and **not** the problematic nature of present-day U.S. foreign and military policies **as** communication. Or, so it appears. So let us examine what is meant by "synchronization" and "strategy for synchronization."[137]

The following characterization is offered.[138] Synchronization requires:

- Coordinating words and deeds, including the active consideration of how our actions and policies will be interpreted by public audiences as an organic part of decisionmaking.
- The recognition that what we do is often more important than what we say because actions have communicative value and send messages.
- Fostering a culture of communication that values this type of synchronization and encourages decision-makers to take the communicative value of actions into account during their decisionmaking. The most senior levels of government must advocate and implement a culture of communication that is reinforced through mechanisms and processes.

This declared necessity of word-deed synchronization or word-deed consistency requires a "strategy for synchronization" which combines several declaratory sentences with suggested methods and means.[139]

- A key lesson we have learned is that actions beyond those managed by the communications community have communicative value and impact. Every action that the United States Government takes sends a message . . .
- Importance of identifying, evaluating, and coordinating the communicative value of actions as a proactive and organic part of planning and decisionmaking . . .
- Ensure strategic goals and messages are well understood at all levels . . .
- Raise awareness about the communicative impact of decisions and actions [and] . . . empha-

size the importance of considering such impacts proactively . . .

- Ensure that forums exist for deliberating these impacts on high-priority issues and coordinating actions with deliberate communication and engagement.

The second base of strategic communication, "deliberate communication and engagement," is characterized as follows:

- A wide range of [USG] programs and activities deliberately focused on understanding, engaging, informing, influencing, and communicating with people through public affairs, public diplomacy, information operations, and other efforts.
- . . . Coordination mechanisms and processes to improve the United States Government's ability to deliberatively communicate and engage with intended audiences.

The "Strategy for Deliberate Communication and Engagement"[140] is comprised of the following:

- Programs and activities focused on communicating and engaging with the public need to be strategic and long-term, not just reactive and tactical.
- *[F]ocus on articulating what the United States is for, not just what we are against. For example, our efforts to communicate and engage with Muslim communities around the world must be defined primarily by a focus on mutual respect and mutual interest, even as we continue to counter violent extremism by focusing on discrediting and delegitimizing violent extremist networks and ideology.* (emphases added)
- Deliberate communication also helps establish the strategic messages against which our actions are often judged by the public, and deliberate engagement helps identify how our actions are being interpreted and perceived.

- It is vital that the United States is not focused solely on one-way communication, which is why we have consciously emphasized the importance of 'engagement' — connecting with, listening to, and building long-term relationships with key stakeholders.[141]

Excepting the italicized bulleted point above — the **single** instance referred to of genuinely substantive interests and policies — the document is an ode to methodology emphasizing the essential need to orchestrate carefully words and actions, and make sure through deliberate engagement this synchronicity may be further enhanced to advance U.S. policies. But, one may ask, **which policies**? Let us reproduce this italicized text and examine it, line by line.

[F]ocus on articulating what the United States is for, not just what we are against. Is not the most telling proof of what a country is really "for" reflected in its policies, which, in turn, reflect vital interests, and ultimately core values? What we are "for" would then translate into the concrete commitments we have made, with blood and treasure, to uphold certain sets of social and political relationships, and not others. What we are "for" is what we promote and defend in domestic policies and in foreign and military policies, diplomatic policies and cultural policies. Is not "what we are for" to be judged based on actions, deeds done, commitments upheld, interests pursued? Or is "what we are for" a reference to the values we claim to uphold, the beliefs we maintain, the intentions we aspire to realize? The vagueness of the phrase "what we are for" serves to remove the harder edge of governments, peoples, militaries, security forces, police, prisons, and states of banishment or permission to live, from view. The same may be asked of its opposite, "what we

are against." We are against oppression? Then what of crushing dictatorships? We value freedom? Then what of imprisoned activists? We value self-determination? Then what about banishment from the political process? In the end, when the bodies and money are counted that "stand for" and "stand against" realities in the world, what should one determine "we are for" and "we are against." This is the very opposite of vague phraseology.

[O]ur efforts to communicate and engage with Muslim communities around the world must be defined primarily by a focus on mutual respect and mutual interest, even as we continue to counter violent extremism by focusing on discrediting and delegitimizing violent extremist networks and ideology. So, we are for "mutual respect" and "mutual interest." But in concrete, substantive, policy terms, what does "mutual respect" and "mutual interest" look like? Respect is demonstrated in actions, policies, and deeds, and quite evident when one believes their humanity, and that of their kinsmen, has been treated in a dignified, honorable, and deserving manner. Respect is earned when one is on the side of actively opposing indignities, ignoble deeds, undeserved oppression, and humiliation. Mutual interests exist when one reciprocates and exchanges a good for a good, and when a common set of ultimate principles unite even persons otherwise quite different, to recognize, cooperate, and identify. Liberty, opportunity, self-determination, sovereignty, dignity, family, development, peace, security, hope, health, wealth, wisdom . . . one can imagine any number of mutual interests that could be shared. But we must get far more concrete, and take into account whether present U.S. policies, based in specific alliances and a certain regime of stability, contain within themselves definite

limits that prohibit, in practice, the kind of respect and mutuality presumed above. If, in fact, a condition of authoritarian denial of rights and freedoms is logically predicated on the United States as guarantor or underwriter, what am I—an Arab, a Muslim, a man—to conclude about the mutuality of our respect, and our interests?

"But I truly do care about you! I believe deeply in the sanctity of life, liberty, and opportunity!" To which a sober response might be:

> But the proof is in your policies, your deeds, and your actions my friend. It is in your alliances, allies, and interests; it is in what you do, not what you say, or say about what you do. Israel, oil, and autocracy, is what I see. And it is I who pays that price, despite the nobility of the values you profess, and despite the very often generous spirit of your people who birthed the concepts I so seek for myself.

Not an insane retort to our baffled strategic communicator, not at all.

The vital significance of U.S. foreign and military policy as a driver of Muslim attitudes and opinions, and not some generic opposition to Americans or American values per se, is also evident in other independent analyses of and commentaries on U.S. strategic communication and public diplomacy. Only a brief selection from a vast literature is presented below.[142] An important 2003 report[143] by the Center for the Study of the American Presidency, in analyzing the nature of the present U.S. credibility problem in the Muslim world, is explicit: This hostility is especially relevant to perceived U.S. support for Israel's unjust policies toward the Palestinians,[144] but it extends well beyond.

[N]egative Muslim attitudes toward the United States are not based on a general dislike of all things American or on a broader anti-Western outlook; nor are they derived from a clash of values brought about by globalization and modernization. Rather, as with anti-American sentiment among many non-Muslims, the principle source is aversion to U.S. policies. . . . [S]kepticism about the U.S role in promoting democracy in Iraq and elsewhere in the Middle East is accompanied by a widespread belief that, while the United States voices support for democratization abroad, it supports autocratic regimes and helps ensure that democracy is denied to many Arabs and Muslims. Despite the broad support for democracy and civil rights in most Muslim countries, large numbers of Muslims believe they lack such basic liberties as fair elections, impartial judicial systems, freedom of the media from government censorship, and freedom to criticize their governments. **The perception that America supports many authoritarian governments, at least indirectly, assists them in the suppression of these rights, especially in the Middle East, fuels anger at the United States, and its policies** (bold in original).[145]

Of the four major weaknesses evident in current public diplomacy efforts to combat anti-Americanism and the U.S. credibility deficit—U.S. policy, too little funds, sparse media, and a trickle of U.S. messaging swamped by a torrent of anti-U.S. messaging—it is U.S. policy which is regarded as decisive:

[T]he (often enormous) impact of U.S. policies easily overwhelms the effects of policy advocacy and other aspects of public diplomacy. The role that U.S. actions abroad, and increasingly at home, play in the formation of public attitudes overseas is far larger than that of U.S. communications with foreign audiences. Public diplomacy has little effect when weighed against American policies that are perceived by foreign audiences to have negative impacts on human rights, the local economy, or domestic politics (bold in original).[146]

A 2003 Report examining public diplomacy, evidencing the key role of policy yet limiting itself to a highly circumscribed mandate, asserts:

> We fully acknowledge that public diplomacy is only part of the picture. Surveys indicate that much of the resentment toward America stems from real conflicts and displeasure with policies, including those involving the Palestinian-Israeli conflict and Iraq. But our mandate is clearly limited to issues of public diplomacy, where we believe a significant new effort is required.[147]

Concluding Thoughts: Formidable Challenges, Formidable Opportunities.

Four conclusions — three obvious, and one counterintuitive — are warranted by the above analysis. Let us consider the three compelling conclusions first. Though communication involves many potential modalities — words, symbols, and images for example — policies, **are also** communication and **as** communication, USG policies are regarded by many analysts and experts and critics alike as **the most persuasive signifier** of genuine motives, intentions, values, and interests.

Second, it is reasonable to conclude that opposition to specific U.S. foreign and military policies deemed unjust, undemocratic, and insensitive to human suffering and human rights — most especially U.S. policies privileging Israel, oil, and autocracy, at the expense of Palestine[148] and broader democratic aspirations — **not** opposition to American values and ideals, is a primary driver of anti-Americanism in the Arab and Muslim world. Though a small selection of reports and analyses was reviewed, a vast literature corroborating this conclusion exists.[149] What we do in, for, and to the Arab and Muslim world — not our values or who we are as a people — fuel moral outrage. Indeed one may argue that it is precisely because we all share the same values — that all people should enjoy freedom and fairness rather than be subject to tyranny and torture — that U.S. policies perceived as underwriting or at least tolerating tyranny and torture are the root cause of this moral outrage.[150]

Third, U.S. policies that undermine U.S. credibility and inspire moral outrage serve to undermine other forms of communication, often designated "strategic communication" and "public diplomacy." Analysts correctly conclude that no amount of lipstick can be put on these pigs that can successfully overwhelm the matter-of-fact experiences and perceptions of vast masses that associate U.S. interests with the subversion of self-determination and social justice in the Arab and Muslim world. If a picture is worth a thousand words, how do actions, let alone a systematic policy maintained over years, convey this? If communication is 80 percent action and 20 percent words and if there is massive divergence between those words and actions, it is no wonder that USG public diplomacy and strategic communication have faltered so badly in the past decade.

One might conclude from the above that the U.S. disadvantage owing to policy commitments is so severe, even crippling, that the attempt to undermine radicalization and recruitment to the AQ terrorist enterprise and vision is a lost cause. But, a surprisingly opposite counterintuitive inference actually recommends itself. What **has** been proven is that current U.S. policies undermine U.S. credibility and inspire moral outrage, and undermine message resonance. What **has not** been proven is that official USG policies furnish evidence of any sort of a specifically anti-Muslim animus, let alone a systematic war against Islam as a religious faith, or against Muslim adherents of that faith. **There is, in short, nothing in the evidence above that proves the United States is a "Crusader" at war with Islam, or that U.S. interests, policies, and values, require that Islam — even in its robust form as an emboldened political Islam that views religion as a matter very much for the public sphere including law, culture, society, and state — be warred against.**

What **has** been proved above is that American policies are at war with American ideals — that our policy and our democratic social justice rhetoric negate one another. American claims to believe in values widely admired throughout the Arab and Muslim world are seen as hollow professions by a hypocritical and compromised superpower whose genuine commitments are evident in its role as ultimate guarantor and military protector of an illegal Israeli occupation and usurpation of Palestinian aspirations, unhindered access to major oil reserves, and the regimes that are supported that make both possible, i.e., conservative and counter-revolutionary autocrats and monarchs, many of whom imprison and banish their democratic — religious or secular — opposition. Still, this is **not a war against Islam**, but a prejudice in favor of a regime of stability guaranteeing a particular status quo in the Occupied Territories and Middle East energy corridors. It is not, then, an abandonment of a war against Islam that is required: quite the contrary. It is simply a rectification of existing policies to bring them into alignment with deeply held **American** ideals.

It is this credibility gap between professed aspirations and self-evident policies that has been the USG's Achilles heel. It undermines all other U.S. efforts to persuade the Muslim world we harbor no enmity. **It also** furnishes the raw materials from which AQ draws its sophisticated terrorist propaganda. As will be shown later, it is AQ's offensive war against all persons — whether autocratic regimes, American civilians or military, or any Muslim who does not embrace AQ's specific modus operandi — that has been successfully represented as a defensive war against the enemies of Allah, Islam, and the broader faith community (umma). How is it that AQ — an offensive revolutionary, insurgent, terroristic Islamist movement combining transnational objectives with pragmatic strategic doctrine — has successfully disabled the world's only superpower from defending itself against the charge that the United States is an implacable foe of Islam; upholds an anti-Muslim status quo; subjects Muslims to barbaric and inhumane treatment throughout the world; and launches wars of occupation, subjugation, and humiliation? To return to Holbrooke's perplexity, but shorn of his unwillingness or inability to seriously examine the moral outrage inspired by USG policies: "How could a mass murderer who publicly praised the terrorists of Sept. 11 be winning the hearts and minds of anyone? How can a man in a cave out communicate the world's leading communications society?"[151]

The second front in the War of Deeds then requires challenging AQ's terroristic propaganda using actual deeds — those of the USG and those of AQ — to determine in fact, that AQ's case may be undermined by a careful review of the evidence. It is to that task that we now turn.

CHALLENGING DEEDS: COUNTERING AL-QAEDA'S TERRORIST PROPAGANDA

> Most, though not all, of the terrorism we face is fueled by a common ideology — a belief by some that Islam is in conflict with the United States, and the West, and that violence against Western targets, including civilians, is justified in pursuit of a larger cause. Of course, this ideology is based on a lie, for the United States is not at war with Islam; and this ideology is rejected by the vast majority of Muslims, who are the most frequent victims of terrorist attacks. Nevertheless, this ideology persists, and in an age in which ideas and images can travel the globe in an instant, our response to terrorism cannot depend on military or law enforcement alone. We need all elements of national power to win the battle of wills and ideas.[152]

The Vital Function of Propaganda in AQ's Anti-American Terrorism.

Propaganda is a key method designed to influence the perception, morale, and will of various target populations. According to the official Department of Defense (DoD) definition, propaganda is "[a]ny form of adversary communication, especially of a biased or misleading nature, designed to influence the opinions, emotions, attitudes, or behavior of any group, in order to benefit the sponsor, directly or indirectly."[153] What is key for our purposes is not that this is adversarial communication, or that it is a form of influence operations, but that AQ's propaganda is dishonest, deceitful, deliberately distorted disinformation designed to incite, inspire, agitate, and shape profoundly erroneous perceptions about USG intentions and actions vis-à-vis Islam and the Muslim world. That the USG suffers from a profound credibility crisis based in unpopular USG policies and actions is disadvantageous enough; consider, then, how this credibility deficit facilitates the work of skilled terrorist propagandists. That is precisely the present conundrum facing those charged with strategic communication and public diplomacy, and it explains our continuing failure to undermine AQ's propaganda juggernaut. It also explains how it is that thousands of persons are being mobilized worldwide to target what they are being told is an implacably evil enemy of Allah that must be neutralized by any means necessary.

The Terrorist Quadrangle: The Role and Function of Terrorist Propaganda as Communication.[154]

AQ's terrorist propaganda is usefully conceptualized as a distinct element of a quadrangle linking political object, propaganda, terrorist attack, and strategic objectives. (See Figure 1.)

Though top-down versus bottom-up processes of radicalization are differentially emphasized by analysts as key to AQ's overall modus operandi,[155] it is this writers' belief that top-down, bottom-up, and interactive dynamics are all in play. Top-down dimensions include: AQ's global media front, sophisticated propaganda mission, assets dedicated to inciting, catalyzing, mobilizing, educating and training; its conspiratorial cellular structure operating within both hostile environments and more friendly radical milieus to identify, target, and recruit potential operators; and, control of sanctuaries (including virtual sanctuaries in cyberspace) permitting training in terrorist techniques, tactics, and methods. Bottom-up dimensions comprise processes of self-radicalization, self-recruitment, and the ever more common

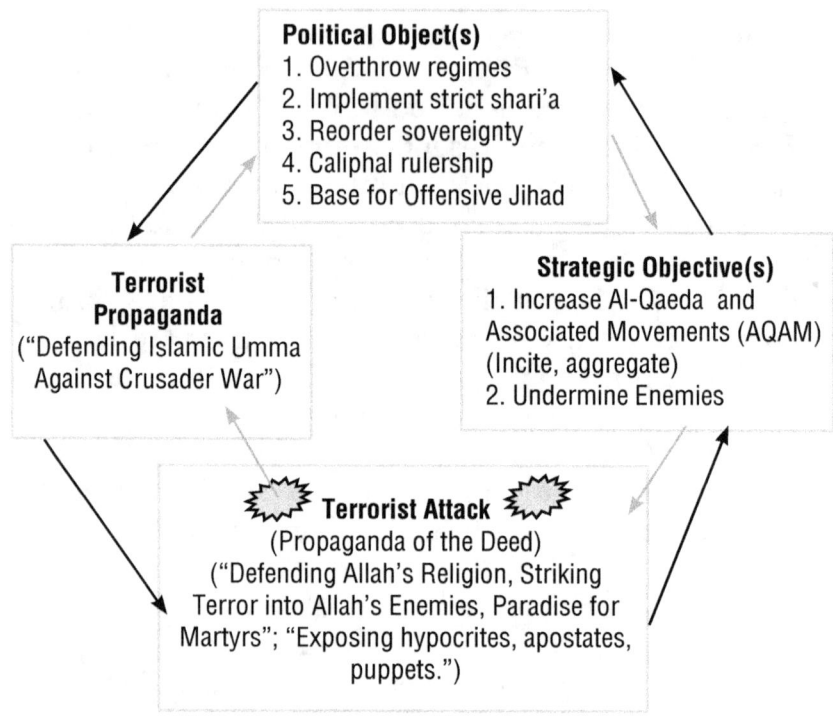

**Figure 1. AQ's Terrorist Quadrangle:
Relations of Political Object, Terrorist Propaganda,
Terror Attacks, and Strategic Objective(s).**

phenomenon of isolated individuals and small groups of acquaintances, friends, or family self-mobilizing once they have been incited or inspired through moral outrage and energized by various social-psychological processes to actively seek out AQ's network.[156] This monograph assumes that both processes operate in highly complex ways and their interaction must always be kept in mind when formulating concrete strategy.

AQ's terrorist propaganda is especially relevant to processes of home-based, home-grown (self-) radicalization and (self-) recruitment to AQ's terrorist modus operandi. Consider, for example, relations between tactical terrorist propaganda, fabricated agitational and inciteful disinformation and the three key psychosocial variables identified earlier; perception, affect, and behavior. In this case, terrorist propaganda is the proximate cause of a distorted perception of USG policies, moral indignation and outrage, and (self-) radicalization and (self-) recruitment to terror. Successful AQ tactical propaganda feeds and nourishes behavioral radicalization by bringing to a white heat feelings of moral outrage based in a perception that the United States is the chief architect and arbiter of an oppressive, unjust power structure crushing their Muslim and sisters. This moral outrage is based on perceptions of social injustice that increase one's susceptibility to accepting the premise that the United States is an implacable enemy of Islam presently engaged in a systematic war against the worldwide Muslim umma; and, that terrorist actions are legitimately directed against the USG, its interests, and its allies. This premise is both amplified and reinforced by the USG credibility crisis, based in a gulf between U.S. ideals and actions. Opposition to U.S. policies includes engaging in activities and finding outlets for securing retribution and justice such as joining ongoing AQ campaigns and finding opportunities to die a *shahid* (martyr). Persons embarking on this path conceive their actions as **justified self-defense** and not **unjustified criminal murder.** They believe they are assisting the oppressed and aggrieved, and fulfilling the general religious obligation within Islam for able-bodied, capable, and knowledgeable persons to assist in whatever ways possible and legal to lift the burdens of injustice and oppression from the shoulders of those presently in the clutches of their anti-Muslim oppressors.

The Critical Function of Counterpropaganda in Countering Insurgent Terrorism.

Deliberate and effective counterpropaganda is deemed essential by analysts and expert practitioners when the USG's very credibility is at stake. It is also used to counter and deflate the agitation, incitement, and mobilization function of propaganda in the AQ terrorist quadrangle.[157] Unfortunately, despite this admittedly critical role, recent changes in the official DoD lexicon have obscured the precise conception and definition of this task. As earlier defined, propaganda is deemed something only adversaries do and is by nature disinformative. It is designed to use fabrications, manipulations, and techniques of influence, to gain advantages for one's own interests at the expense of rationally conceived objective truth. Given this negative function, how, then, can **counter**propaganda be conceived?

PSYOP, recently renamed Military Information Support Operations (MISO), was until recently the official name given by the DoD to the activity most resembling what one would imagine to be USG-based propaganda.[158] A most terse definition is offered by U.S. Army Special Operations: "The mission of PSYOP is to influence the behavior of foreign TA's [target audiences] to support U.S. national objectives."[159] This is not significantly different from the definition of propaganda cited above:

> [a]ny form of adversary communication, especially of a biased or misleading nature, designed to influence the opinions, emotions, attitudes, or behavior of any group, in order to benefit the sponsor, directly or indirectly.

Let us now juxtapose the older, fuller PSYOP definition with its MISO replacement term.

[PSYOP]: Planned operations to convey selected information and indicators to foreign audiences to influence their emotions, motives, objective reasoning, and ultimately the behavior of foreign governments, organizations, groups, and individuals. The purpose of psychological operations is to induce or reinforce foreign attitudes and behavior favorable to the originator's objectives.[160]

[MISO]: Planned operations to convey selected information and indicators to foreign audiences to influence their emotions, motives, objective reasoning, and ultimately the behavior of foreign governments, organizations, groups, and individuals in a manner favorable to the originator's objectives.[161]

How Counterpropaganda Differs from Propaganda or PSYOP.

The function of propaganda, PSYOP or MISO, when stripped of euphemistic labels and spin, is to manipulate target audiences using known psychological techniques so that one's own interests are more likely to be realized. It is part of the broader art and science of influence operations, and deemed a vital dimension of warfare to the extent that attacking enemy morale, will, attitudes, perceptions, and emotions, is a key means of influencing an adversary's behavior. Counterpropaganda as I conceive it, however, does **not** involve countering adversary propaganda with one's own. Counterpropaganda is the refutation of fiction by fact, not the opposing of one fiction to another.

In this monograph, counterpropaganda denotes the logical and factual refutation of an adversary's propaganda, where propaganda is identical to fabrication; disinformation; and deceitful, distorted, and dishonest communication. This refutation must be truthful, verifiable, credible, and subject to proof based on tests of external reliability performed by objective observers. Its chief objective in the war against AQ is first, to factually assess and evaluate the USG's and AQ's **actual deeds** in relation to the Arab and Islamic worlds; and then, on the basis of such, formulate deliberate counter-AQ information warfare strategy.

Conceived in this manner, counterpropaganda's nearest relative is countering adversarial disinformation, or "counterdisinformation." This latter term fails to signify that it is propaganda, and specifically terrorist propaganda, rather than information, that is at issue in the terrorist quadrangle. Disinformation may be a subset of terrorist tasks, but the unique properties of propaganda are not conveyed by the sanitized term "information" any more than the term "Military Information Support Operations" accurately conveys its PSYOP function as military propaganda in support of national objectives.[162]

ELEMENTS OF A COMPREHENSIVE USG COUNTERPROPAGANDA COUNTEROFFENSIVE

In what follows, the chief elements of a counterpropaganda counteroffensive against AQ are outlined. Beginning with a discussion and conception of influence operations, contemporary war and warfare, and the instruments of national power, attention is then turned to the key tasks required of the two fronts in the War of Deeds.

Influence Operations, Contemporary War, and Warfare.

Influence Operations.

Counterpropaganda must first be conceptualized in relation to a broader concept of contemporary war, warfare, and influence operations. Influence operations are those whose ultimate goal is to influence behavior in a manner favorable to its sponsor.[163] Influence operations address the full range of potential variables, including traditional kinetic means, that affect motivation, attitudes, beliefs, and ultimately behaviors.

Contemporary War and Warfare.

Influence is the chief objective of newer conceptions of war and warfare achieved via a vast terrain of social, technological, cultural, political, financial, and psychological methods and means. Today's battlefield is not militarized and kinetic, but can be broadened to include a virtually inexhaustible and unrestricted mass of energy to be deployed in the service of policy.[164] In relation to this concept of war and warfare, a recent author suggests the utility of discarding "conceptions of war and warfare that include only the traditional kinetic sense and instead think about forms of conflict that do not take lives or cause damage."[165] Consider, for example, the following conception:

> What is significant is that all of these warfighting means, along with their corresponding applications, that have entered, are entering, or will enter, the ranks of warfighting means in the service of war, have al-

ready begun to quietly change the view of warfare held by all of mankind. Faced with a nearly infinitely diverse array of options to choose from, why do people want to enmesh themselves in a web of their own making and select and use means of warfare that are limited to the realm of force of arms and military power? Methods that are not characterized by the use of the force of arms, nor even by the presence of casualties and bloodshed, are just as likely to facilitate the successful realization of the war's goals, if not more so. As a matter of course, this prospect has led to revision of the statement that 'war is politics with bloodshed' [Clausewitz, Mao] and in turn has also led to a change in the hitherto set view that warfare prosecuted through force of arms is the ultimate means of resolving conflict [Clausewitz, also p. 7, 36]. Clearly, it is precisely the means employed that has enlarged the concept of warfare. Moreover, the enlargement of the concept of warfare has, in turn, resulted in an enlargement of the realm of war-related activities. . . . Any war that breaks out tomorrow or further down the road will be characterized by warfare in the broad sense — a cocktail mixture of warfare prosecuted through the force of arms and warfare that is prosecuted by means other than the force of arms. The goal of this kind of warfare will encompass more than merely 'using means that involve the force of arms to force the enemy to accept one's own will' [Clausewitz]. Rather, the goal should be 'to use all means whatsoever — means that involve the force of arms and means that do not involve the force of arms, means that involve military power and means that do not involve military power, means that entail casualties and means that do not entail casualties — to force the enemy to serve one's interests'.[166]

74

From M, to Diplomatic, Informational, Military, and Economic (DIME), to DIMEFIL, to DICEFILM: On the Eight Instruments of National Power.

A counterpropaganda campaign directed against AQ must also take into account the full range of elements and instruments of national power brought to bear on those three chief variables enabling terrorist actions: subjective motivation, subjective and objective capability, and objective opportunity. These eight major instruments of national power—diplomatic, informational, cyber, economic, financial, intelligence, legal, military—arrayed against these three variables are presented in Figure 2.

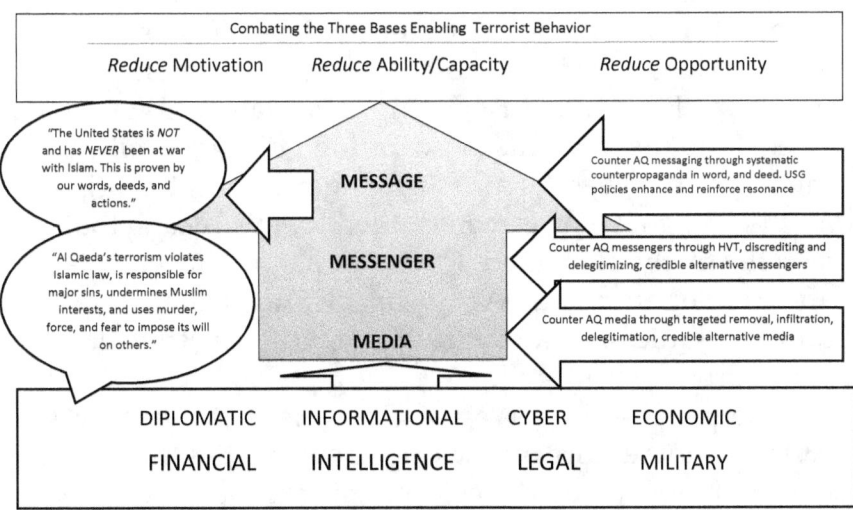

Figure 2. Elements of a Comprehensive USG Counterpropaganda Counteroffensive to Combat Radicalization and Recruitment to AQ Terrorism.

As one can see in Figure 2, inclusion of the cyber (C) domain extends the principal instruments of national power beyond their originally-conceptualized four (DIME), and more recent extension to seven by adding the financial, intelligence, and legal domains (DIMEFIL or MIDLIFE),[167] to eight in order to fully capture the means employed in the digital revolution manifest in cyberspace.[168] Well attested in recent doctrine and analyses,[169] and obviously central to the domain of countering AQ propaganda, this essential element of national power must now be given its proper recognition.[170]

Countering AQ Propaganda:
The Primacy of the War of Deeds.

Next, I briefly describe the two key fronts in a War of Deeds designed to counter AQ terrorist propaganda. By deftly organizing a sustained War of Deeds and, as a result, eviscerating AQ's credibility, the nexus between terrorist propaganda and terrorist acts (see Figure 1) is severed. Ideally, this means that an effectively sustained USG campaign can cripple and render impotent AQ's capacity to incite moral outrage, radicalize, and earn new recruits as so-called vanguard of a besieged.

The premise of a War of Deeds is that defeating AQ does not require mimicking enemy tactics through manipulation of evidence, spin, tricks or deceptive arts of any sort. Instead it requires the confident deployment of human reason and martialing of genuine evidence that can in the long run triumph over fabrications, propaganda, disinformation, and AQ's violent offensive war against all who disagree with its political objectives, especially its terrorist modus operandi. Veracity and credibility rather than perfection of USG deeds is key to a War of Deeds. An objective, factual investigation of U.S. actions will **not** confirm any kind of Crusader war against Islam. Reason and evidence, duly combined, will reveal tractable clashes of interests; intracivilizational fault lines over religion and state; intercivilizational dialogue and conflict over core conceptions, and even potential intercivilizational conflicts, and even occasional clashes. It will **not** confirm, even remotely, however, a Crusader war against Islam. Undoubtedly some elements within U.S. society **do** seek a neo-Crusader agenda. This includes a Christian Zionist, Zionist, and neo-conservative political coalition which denies the policy roots of anti-U.S. animus. Instead it argues exclusively for war-footing against a supposedly ignoble Islamic or jihadist enemy found in virtually all guises — including the bogeyman of the Muslim Brotherhood. Undoubtedly, this extremely powerful political coalition functions within the United States to prejudice policies and foreign relations.[171] Despite this, however, no rational analysis of USG policies, deeds, and actions confirms that it is official or unofficial USG policy to wage war on Islam, Muslims, or the Arab Muslim world.

Countering AQ Messengers and Media.

A counterpropaganda counteroffensive along the lines of the War of Deeds suggested here has as its chief goal using three key elements — the media, messengers, and messages — to undermine motivation via incitement to moral outrage, and thereby radicalization and recruitment to AQ terrorism. Let us begin with the latter two first. As Figure 2 describes, countering AQ propaganda requires countering AQ's **mes-**

sengers. The specific methods, tactics, techniques, and procedures (TTPs) specific to this objective include: eliminating AQ propagandists through deliberate targeting in ongoing HVT campaigns (e.g., Anwar al-Awlaki and Abu Yahya al-Libi); infiltrating AQ oriented internet chat rooms and fora with the objective of discrediting and delegitimizing AQ's messengers by countering disinformation, exploiting contradictions, and exposing fallacies; using the weapons of ridicule, satire, and character assassination to destroy messenger credibility;[172] finally, attempts to recruit alternative messengers whose bona fide credibility may be leveraged to further damage AQ's jihadist brand.[173] Second, AQ **media** must be countered, using such methods and TTPs as targeted removal, infiltration, delegitimation of AQ media and sources, and legitimizing alternative credible media sources that effectively challenge AQ's propagandistic assertions.

*Countering AQ's Two Greatest Lies Using a
War of Deeds.*

Destroying AQ's messengers and media, and enhancing U.S. media and messenger credibility is necessary, but insufficient. The knock-out blow, I believe, results when the USG overtly, directly, and effectively challenges and refutes AQ's most essential **messages** in a War of Deeds. As Figure 3 indicates, there are two vital "great lies" that AQ starkly juxtaposes—"The U.S. Crusader" and "The Islamic Defender"—that must be countered effectively in this War of Deeds. To refute these great lies requires two countermessages. Message 1: "The United States is NOT and has NEVER been at war with Islam. This is proven by our words, deeds, actions, and policies." Message 2: "The

Al-Qaeda terrorist entity is a violent criminal enterprise that violates Islamic law, is responsible for major sins, undermines Muslim interests, and uses murder, force, and fear to impose its will on others." Each message, when combined in a sustained campaign, counters these great lies using concrete facts, actual policies, actions, and deeds associated with the USG and AQ. To facilitate this task, let us juxtapose AQ's two greatest lies (propaganda) and the USG messages (counterpropaganda) required to refute them:

AQ Great Lie #1: The United States is engaged in a Crusader-Zionist war against Islam and the Muslim world.	USG Refutation of Great Lie #1: The United States is NOT and has NEVER been at war with Islam. This is proven by our words, actions, deeds, and policies.
AQ Great Lie #2: AQ is fighting a defensive jihad to protect the Muslim umma and Islam from an offensive Crusader-Zionist War.	USG Refutation of Great Lie #2: The AQ criminal terrorist enterprise violates Islamic law, commits major sins, undermines Muslim interests, and uses murder, force, and fear to impose its will on others.

Figure 3. Method for Refuting AQ's Big Lies.

Method for Refuting AQs Big Lie #1.

AQ's first big lie—The U.S. Crusader War against Islam—rests on five fabrications alleged as matters of indisputed empirical fact, which have been central to its earliest declarations of war in 1996 and 1998, justifying the killing of Americans, civilian and military, and repeatedly throughout subsequent communiques.[174] Each of these fabrications may be treated as premises, and AQ's first big lie as the alleged conclusion.

Premise 1: *The Murderer of Muslim Millions.* The United States is directly or indirectly responsible for the murder of millions of Muslim men, women, and children.

Premise 2: *The Apostate Installer-Defender.* The United States rules directly or indirectly through anti-Muslim apostate governments it installs, maintains, and defends throughout the Muslim world.

Premise 3: *The Imperialist-Exploiter.* The United States maintains a purely imperialist, exploitative, and predatory relationship to Middle East oil supplies and is pillaging the wealth of the Muslim world.

Premise 4: *The Aggressive Permanent Occupier.* U.S.-led military operations in Afghanistan, and earlier Iraq, and at present throughout the Muslim world, are militant offensive wars motivated by a desire to destroy Islam, permanently occupy Muslim lands, or rule indirectly through anti-Muslim apostate governments.

Premise 5: *The U.S.-Zionist Plot to Create Israel to Divide and Destroy the Umma.* The state of Israel was created as part of a Western colonial plot to establish a Crusader-Zionist beachhead at the center of the Muslim world to divide, weaken, and eventually uproot Islam from Palestine and the greater Middle East. Steadfast U.S. support for Israel is motivated primarily by that anti-Muslim colonial intention.

These five fabrications have gone essentially unchallenged to the present day. Whether refuting them is considered the equivalent of refuting holocaust deniers or 9/11 truthers, or flat-earthers, or martialing facts has lost out to the so-called "battle of ideas," not taking these as deadly serious in the context of the USG credibility deficit, over the course of a decade, has permitted fictions to become living legends with predictably deadly consequences.[175] If one chooses, one can also use concepts derived from framing theory[176] to perceive these five fabrications as alleged empirical nodes supporting AQ's anti-American "injustice frame." By effectively countering these fabrications, one obliterates the supporting tissue of this injustice frame that inspires moral outrage and animates recruits.

It is not a far stretch to see how an angry, newly-inspired, morally-outraged young recruit could be led through the lens of AQ's sophisticated propaganda to see present U.S. policy commitments as motivated primarily by anti-Muslim animus. Instead of privileging access to oil reserves, the United States is a pillager-exploiter (Premise 3). Instead of a very powerful lobby in defense of Israel's security and expansion, which in effect, permits an illegal occupation, settlement, and continuing humiliation of the Palestinian people to persist, the United States has an ultimate divide and conquer strategy (Premise 5). Instead of a policy that privileges conservative, stability-promoting anti-democratic autocrats and monarchs, the United States is an apostate installer-defender (Premise 2).

Objective, factual, historical evidence is all that is required to refute AQ's five fabrications (premises) and first big lie (conclusion). A sound argument consists of true and relevant premises from which a conclusion necessarily follows. It will be essential that such facts are considered credible, thus requiring credible messengers and media, for their legitimacy.

While U.S. analysts are certainly capable of discovering, arranging, and communicating such facts, a curiously powerful messenger and source of credibility should also be leveraged: committed Islamists whose militant bona fides are unassailable, but who offer decisive evidence refuting AQ's fabricated propagandistic history of U.S. involvement in the Arab and Muslim world. Consider the following realistic rather than propagandistic account provided by leaders of the Egyptian Islamic Group (Al Gama'a al-Islamiyya) — opposed on grounds of principle, legality, and pragmatics to AQ's terroristic modus operandi — of U.S. core strategic interests and their implications for U.S. relations with the Islamic world.

> The conception that America is waging a Crusade against Muslims is not true. . . . in the worst of cases [one can say that] at times there have been American policies that have had a religious dimension in opposing some — and not all — of the Islamic world's causes. [The fact that this is not a Crusade] explains America's positive stand in support of the Afghani mujahideen in their fight against the Soviet occupation, and [America's] positive stand [against] the ethnic cleansing operation against the Muslims of Bosnia and Herzegovina and in the province of Kosovo. Likewise, the conception that America aimed to bring down the Taliban regime in Afghanistan and could not have been deterred from doing so is not true. Reality attests to the fact that America attempted to come to terms with the Taliban regime in order to realize common strategic goals . . . and these attempts to come to an understanding ran up against the Al-Qaeda organization's actions, which were launched from Afghanistan and targeted America, and which the Taliban authorities did not restrain.[177] . . . America at that time was looking for new strategies for a new century, and if the Front [i.e., Al-Qaeda] and other interpreters of Islam had adopted serious Islamic strategy that would have given consideration to American interests together with Islamic interests, this would have prevented the continuation of this war or [at least] would have kept it from taking on a comprehensive nature.[178]

An earlier work authored by this same organization deeply critical of AQ[179] provides an even broader, in-depth account and rendering of key U.S. objectives vis-à-vis the Muslim world.

> In this chapter, the leaders of the Egyptian Al-Jama'ah Al-Islamiyah review and assess strategy on the issues of the Muslim world in an attempt to answer several important questions necessitated by current world events: Did U.S. strategy target the Muslim world or not? Are we in a state of self-defense that allows Al-Qaida to do what it wants? The authors argue that Al-Qaida's interpretation of U.S. strategy is not accurate but is characterized, as they say, with unfairness. The authors say that any observer of U.S. strategy will find that the prime mover of this strategy is interests and not the religious factor. This explains many major events in which the United States appeared to be supportive of some Islamic issues, such as support for the Afghan jihad in 1979 against the Soviet presence. The leaders of Al-Jama'ah Al-Islamiyya divide this U.S. strategy into three phases. The first starts with the end of the First World War in 1945 [sic] until the end of the Cold War in December 1991 with the collapse of the Soviet Union. The second phase begins in 1991 until the [1998] proclamation of the World Front to Combat the Jews and the Crusaders [by AQ] and the start of operations against the United States. The third phase stretches from 11 September 2001 events to [the present] date. At the end of their evaluation of the U.S. strategy, the authors conclude that Al-Qa'ida's strategy was one of the most important factors that hastened the formulation of this U.S. strategy that is negative toward the Muslim world.[180]

Method for Refuting AQs Big Lie #2.

The War of Deeds is especially appropriate for refuting AQ's propaganda that it is **the vanguard** fighting a **defensive** war against a Crusader-Zionist alliance. The five premises similarly service this conclusion; exposing the fabricated nature of those premises suffices then, to render this conclusion invalid.

Whereas the previous task requires **refuting lies** that radically impugn USG credibility, the task here is **confirming facts** that impugn AQ's credibility. Because AQ fights in the name of Islam and defends its actions in terms of a strict, classical interpretation of the shari'a regulating the lawful waging of the jihad, radically impugning AQ's credibility means exposing not only its empirical fabrications, but its legal-moral violations, i.e., sinfulness.

Jurisprudence and Fiqh al-Jihad.

Far from fighting a defensive jihad against Crusaders, AQ is **in fact** a criminal terrorist enterprise that is guilty of egregious violations of Islamic law, including the commission of major sins such as: intentional homicide, deemed unpardonable on the Day of Judgment; imprudent sacrificing of Muslim interests throughout the world; and violating generally expected norms of humane conduct by using murder, force, and fear to impose its will on others. Let us consider each in turn.

The jihad of the sword (*jihad bis saif*)[181] is strictly regulated by classical sources of orthodox religious authority. AQ claims to uphold faithfully the classical shari'a of lawful jihad by strictly adhering to the path of *al salaf al salih* (the path followed by the "righteous" ancestors). These earliest companions of and successors to Prophet Muhammad furnish for genuine salafists **the** normative ideal of righteous intention and conduct, including the conduct of jihad. AQ also

84

claims to strictly abide by an established body of law (*fiqh*) transmitted by classical religious scholar-jurists prescribing and regulating *jihad fi sabil Allah* (jihad in the path of Allah). The most damaging case against AQ arises when these shari'a sources are marshaled to persuasively demonstrate that absolutely forbidden (*haram*) violations have been perpetrated. Should AQ's terroristic modus operandi demonstrate discontinuity, innovation, and forbidden acts that contradict Prophet Muhammad's "sunna" — though marketed in AQ apologetics as **the** "salafi-jihadi" path — its violation of the classical jihad would be proven, and its legitimacy impaled.[182]

Devastating cases against AQ's violations of *fiqh al-jihad* exist, and should be fully leveraged to prove that AQ is guilty of murderous jihadism and has in fact innovated a doctrine of "killing in masse" predicated on engaging in many legally/morally forbidden acts. Among these forbidden acts are: the killing of several categories of person — Muslim and non-Muslim — whose blood, reputation, and property are strictly protected under Islamic law; violation of the shari'a regulating the use of human shields in combat; violation of the law of retribution or *lex talionis*; violation of laws forbidding treachery and the breaking of covenants; and killing persons on the basis of nationality.[183]

Prudence and Muslim Interests.

Prudential critiques are also key to obliterating AQ's propaganda, which asserts it fights on behalf of Muslims and is essential to the defense of Islamic lands and power. To the contrary, AQ's murderous jihadism is responsible for a host of consequences.

What follows is a short list. AQ has caused the fall of the Taliban regime. It has besmirched a great faith, Islam, by equating it in the minds of a broader public with barbaric terror. AQ's actions have created greater support for a securitized environment that has placed Muslims, and others, in a far more precarious position vis-à-vis the free exercise of civil liberties, than previously. AQ has de-legitimized the broader Islamist resurgence in the minds of a broader public seeking along with other actors, to democratically contest existing unpopular, autocratic regimes. *Fiqh al-jihad* requires that the decision to wage the jihad of the sword take into account the probability of success, the relative benefits and costs to Islam of the choice to use force, and takes full advantage of many other permissible and recommendable means that may be used to spread the worship and Word of Allah.[184]

Ethics and Human Morality.

AQ's use of murder, force, and fear — the essence of its modus operandi as a criminal terrorist organization — denies human individuals, Muslim and non-Muslim, the right to choose alternative paths and means for realizing aspirations in the contemporary world. Terror as a fear-generating tool designed to instill dread in order to attain power over others undermines the fundamental sense of personal security: a security without which the exercise of freedom and liberty is not possible.[185] AQ is, at its root, in permanent war with any and all Muslims and non-Muslims, who dissent from its path of murderous jihadism.

Despite opposition to USG policies, overwhelming majorities of Muslim and non-Muslim alike view terrorism as a morally reprehensible means for achieving power over others. They view nonviolent, democratic means as a superior means of fighting for one's rights and freedoms, as well as for selecting representatives who are replaceable and accountable to the governed. These overwhelming majorities do not view democracy as a substitute religion involving a worshipful relation or replacement of an Almighty by man. Rather, they view democracy as the most effective means of ensuring that man, as a morally challenged being fraught with vices and temptations and desires, be subject to accountable laws and governments, and not the tyranny of an unchosen dictator, or self-appointed vanguard. The "take away" message for the USG of this most American of ideals — self-determination under an elected and accountable government under law — seems obvious. "Better relations with Arab societies as a whole," Jamal Amay of Princeton's Department of Politics, recently asserts:[186]

> will require reconsidering U.S. policies that ignore the preferences of ordinary citizens, such as continuing to back authoritarian regimes, increasing drone attacks in the region, and supporting the ongoing Israeli occupation of the West Bank. A carefully constructed foreign policy will have to take into account the preferences of millions of Arabs across the region. . . . There is no evidence of some deep and durable Arab hatred of the United States. . . . [C]itizens across the region recognize that there is much to gain from closer ties to the United States. A carefully designed U.S. foreign policy should ensure that the United States' geostrategic plans incorporate, rather than alienate, those citizens.[187]

The "take away" message for AQ is also clear. AQ's insurgent terror is now, and into an indefinite but certain future, in irreconcilable conflict with this vast majority's sense of decency, morality, and its chosen path forward. Imploding from within, and marginalized from without, AQ shall in time meet the fate—oblivion—of every known terrorist enterprise. Having wreaked havoc now for nearly a quarter century, it is well time for those possessed of facts, to fight AQ's fabrications. The time for a determined, systematic counterpropaganda counteroffensive fought along the lines suggested above, has arrived.

IMPLICATIONS FOR STRATEGY

Ways, Means, and Ends.

Strategy entails that one specify the **way** in which **means** are used to accomplish **ends**.[188] The **end** specified in in this monograph is the second strategic objective outlined in the *9/11 Commission Report*: countering radicalization and recruitment to AQ. The **way** is the concept or method for achieving that strategic objective. In this case, I am suggesting that U.S. strategists use a unique way/methodology: Fighting the War of Deeds. This methodology emphasizes the communicative nature, function, and value of policies, deeds, and actions as drivers of anti-Americanism in the Arab and Muslim world. This method is offered as a distinct supplement, complement, or most likely substitute, for what I deem a mostly ill-advised effort to craft persuasive messaging using public diplomacy, strategic communication, or other persuasive arts that do not begin with and leverage the power of deeds.

The **means** suggested involve all eight instruments of national power described above. If policy **is** communication, each of these instruments must function in harmony to undermine AQ's two greatest lies. A range of agencies and personnel are focused on countering radicalization and recruitment to AQ, and "means" therefore applies to all organizational, financial, and personnel-based resources that must be deployed to realize this objective.

Strategic Validity.

The validity of a strategy requires that it accomplish its desired strategic effect (suitability), is backed by sufficient resources (sustainability), and is deemed legitimate, relative to costs and benefits, among relevant publics (acceptability). Assuming resource sufficiency, I here address the first and third elements.

Suitability. The analysis above confirms the resounding emphasis — across a range of experts, literature, reports, and political orientations — of the critical significance of deeds as communication. The methodology of Fighting the War of Deeds is therefore grounded in known facts and experience regarding the variety of modes available in persuasive communication, and the suitability/efficacy of deeds as chief among them. The War of Deeds is especially suited for the present propaganda-rich environment in which countering radicalization and recruitment to AQ among morally indignant, home-based and home-grown terrorist self-starters has become critical. The overriding emphasis on perceptions of U.S. injustice toward the Muslim world among this population requires that policies speak loudly and powerfully enough to quell doubts and undermine AQ's viral reach.

Acceptability. The War of Deeds is likely to meet resistance among certain sub-populations who consider themselves beneficiaries of present U.S. foreign and military policy in the Arab and Muslim world. It is also likely to meet resistance among a broader American populace who may believe that carefully examining U.S. foreign and military policy, and perceptions of that policy amount to "rewarding" terrorism. It will require a determined effort to prove that, in fact, one may develop new understandings without sanctioning terrorism or AQ's murderous jihadism, as a legitimate means of addressing existing injustices. Taking the initiative to clarify and define present policies and their implications for future relations with the Arab and Muslim world is highly advisable; fighting an ill-defined "war of ideas" as a reaction to AQ's bloody provocations and perfidious methods, is not.

Strategic Risks.

Strategic risk must consider the probable consequences of success and failure of a given strategy. It asks the question: Given this unique strategy, and in the context of this strategic environment, what strategic effects are likely to be created by the implementation of this strategy? Many other questions must also be raised: How will this strategy affect the present equilibrium among actors? What potential unintended effects, and second- and third-order effects, exist?

CONCLUSION

I will close this monograph on a note of genuine humility and state that I must leave to genuine strategists the careful, methodical evaluation of these potential risks arising from vigorously fighting a War of Deeds as proposed here. It is my firm conviction that the United States of America is — owing to its youthful

18th century provenance and pioneering role as creator, defender, and promoter of democratic ideals—on the right side of history, while AQ faces inexorable implosion and marginalization and an inevitable demise. Its global ambitions, murderous methods, and arrogant pretensions condemn it to wreaking havoc and parasitizing chaos. I firmly believe that the long process of reconstructing states, legitimacy, and boundaries now unfolding throughout the fermenting Arab and Muslim world naturally benefits the United States, and we, them. We are both, we are all, aspiring to realize, and not negate, functioning, productive, sociopolitical, socioeconomic, and sociocultural orders. For those reasons, it seems to me that the risk of not acting boldly to proclaim an enduring alliance with this emergent order and its Sunni majority is far greater than the risks we face, as nation after nation deposes its autocrats and dictators and possibly also its monarchs. Must we, having failed to develop a post-autocratic, post-Cold War vision, vacillate between embracing the autocrats who guarantee short-term regime stability and the democrats—Muslim and secular—who seek to dethrone them? I believe a natural, long-term alliance and dialogue of civilizations is in the making and that possibly the greatest risk of all is failing to understand that the older algorithm—oil, Israel, and autocracy—does not give way to a fuller conception. One, in short, that does not require lipstick.

ENDNOTES

1. Scott Shane, "Suspects With Foot in 2 Worlds, Perhaps Echoing Plots of Past," *The New York Times*, April 2013, available from *www.nytimes.com/2013/04/21/us/boston-suspects-confused-identities-and-conflicting-loyalties.html?pagewar*.

2. President of the United States, *National Strategy for Counterterrorism*, June 2011, p. 17.

3. Kim Cragin and Scott Gerwehr, *Dissuading Terror: Strategic Influence and the Struggle Against Terrorism*, Santa Monica, CA: RAND, 2005, p. iii.

4. Paul Kamolnick, *Delegitimizing Al-Qaeda: A Jihad-Realist Approach*, Carlisle, PA: Strategic Studies Institute, U.S. Army War College, March 2012.

5. Office of the President, *National Security Strategy*, Washington, DC: The White House, May 2010, pp. 4, 19-22, available from *www.whitehouse.gov/sites/default/files/rss_viewer?national_security?strategy.pdf*; Office of the President, *National Strategy for Countering Terrorism*, Washington, DC: The White House, June 2011, pp. 1, 3, available from *www.whitehouse.gov/sites/default/files/counterterrorism_strategy.pdf*; United States Department of Defense, *Quadrennial Defense Review Report*, Washington, DC: United States Institute of Peace, February 2010, pp. v, 6, 15, available from *www.defense.gov/qdr/QDR%20as%20of%2026JAN10%200700.pdf*; Quadrennial Defense Review Independent Panel, *The QDR in Perspective: Meeting America's National Security Needs in the 21st Century, Final Report of the Quadrennial Defense Review Independent Panel*, Corrected Advance Copy, 2010, Washington, DC: United States Institute of Peace, p. 26; U.S. Department of Defense, *Sustaining U.S. Global Leadership: Priorities for 21st Century Defense*, Washington, DC: Department of Defense (DoD), January 2012, p. 4, available from *www.defense.gov/news/Defense_Strategic_Guidance.pdf*; President Barack Obama, "The Future of our Fight Against Terrorism," Speech at National Defense University, Washington, DC, May 23, 2013, esp. pp. 1-2, available from *www.guardian.co.uk/world/2013/may/23/obama-drones-guantanamo-speech-text/print*.

6. See for example, Peter Bergen, "Time to declare victory: al Qaeda is defeated," June 27, 2012, available from *security.blogs.cnn.com*; Peter Bergen, *The Longest War: The Enduring Conflict between America and Al-Qaeda*, London, UK: Free Press, 2011, esp. Chap. 12, "Al-Qaeda 2.0 (pp. 197-213) and Chap. 20, "The Long Hunt" (pp. 335-351); Peter Bergen, "From Benghazi to Boston: the state of the jihad," available from *www.cnn.com*; Peter Bergen, "Bush's

war on terror is over," May 26, 2013, available from *www.cnn.com*. In this latter piece Bergen argues for a "whack a mole" approach to al-Qaeda (AQ) affiliates, asserts that "big Al Qaeda" is on its way out, and that though deradicalization remains an important task, it is time to end this "longest war," and U.S. Government (USG) attempts to define this as a task of global reach under the auspices of an unending authorization, and using illicit methods. See also Stephanie Gaskell, "Al Qaeda on 'Life Support'," July 16, 2013, available from *www.defenseone.com/threats/2013/07/al-qaeda-life-support/66809*; Fawaz A. Gerges, *The Rise and Fall of Al-Qaeda*, London, UK, and New York: Oxford University Press, 2011, esp. pp. 189-192, 200-202; Michael G. Vickers, Under Secretary of Defense for Intelligence, "The Evolution of Al-Qaeda and Associated Movements," Transcript prepared from Audio File Entitled "110913-opening-panel-with-Vickers [Being at Audio Counter 04:31:32-4:46:57], in Joseph J. Simons, Adjunct, CRC, "Ten Years Later: Insights on al-Qaeda's Past and Future through Captured Records: A Conference Report," January 27, 2012; Army Sgt. 1st Class Tyrone C. Marshall, Jr., "Military Has Crushed al-Qaida Since 9/11, Official Says," February 8, 2012, available from *www.defense.gov*; Kenneth Ross, "The war against al-Qaeda is over," *The Washington Post*, August 2, 2013.

7. See for example, Frud Bezhan, "The Rise of Al-Qaeda 2.0," July 24, 2013, available from *www.theatlantic.com/international/archive/2013/07/the-rise-of-al-qaeda-20/278059*; Max Boot, "Al-Qaeda's Resurgence," *Commentary*, October 11, 2012, available from *www.commentarymagazine.com/2012/10/11/al-qaedas-resurgence/*; Martha Crenshaw, "Assessing the Al-Qa'ida Threat to the United States," *CTC Sentinel*, Vol. 3, No. 1, January 2010, pp. 6-9; Brian Michael Jenkins, "Is the War on Terror Over? Not Yet," Santa Monica, CA: The RAND Corporation, April 30, 2012; Peter Bergen and Bruce Hoffman, "Assessing the Terrorist Threat," Report of the National Security Preparedness Group, September 10, 2012; Seth G. Jones, "Re-Examining the Al Qa'ida Threat to the United States," Testimony presented before the House Foreign Affairs Committee, Subcommittee on Terrorism, Nonproliferation, and Trade, "Global al Qaeda: Affiliates, Objectives, and Future Challenges," July 18, 2013; Seth G. Jones, "Resurgence of al Qaeda," Santa Monica, CA: The Rand Corporation, October 16, 2013; Seth G. Jones, "Al Qaeda is Far From Defeated," *The Wall Street Journal*, April 29, 2012; Seth G. Jones, "Think Again: Al Qaeda," *Foreign Policy*, April 23, 2012, available from *www.foreignpolicy.com/*

articles/2012/04/23/think_again_al_qaeda; Seth G. Jones, "Difficult Questions on Today's Terrorist Threat," Santa Monica, CA: The RAND Corporation, October 22, 2012, available from *www.rand. org/commentary/2012/10/22/RAND.html*; Thomas Joscelyn, "Global al Qaeda: Affiliates, objectives, and future challenges," *Long War Journal*, July 18, 2013, available from *www.longwarjournal.org/archives/2013/07/global_al_qaeda_affi-print.php*; Anna Mulrine, "Al Qaeda growing, but less focused on US, study finds," *Christian Science Monitor*, July 22, 2013, available from *www.csmonitor.com*; David Gartenstein-Ross, "Reports of Al Qaeda's Death Have Been Greatly Exaggerated," *Foreign Policy*, October 3, 2012, available from *www.foreignpolicy.com*; Con Coughlin, "The war isn't over yet," *London Sunday Telegraph*, August 4, 2013, available from *www.telegraph.co.uk/news/worldnews/al-qaeda/10222159/This-war-isnt-over-yet.html*; Juan Zarate and Thomas Sanderson, "Terrorism's shifting face," *The Washington Post*, August 5, 2013, op-ed, available from *www.washingtonpost.com*; Editorial Board, "Wishful thinking on the war on terror," *The Washington Post*, August 5, 2013, available from *www.washingtonpost.com*; Bill Roggio, "Al Qaeda isn't dead, FBI director says," *Long War Journal*, August 23, 2013, available from *www.longwarjournal.org*. FBI Director Robert Mueller is quoted: "We are seeing dialogue between core Al Qaeda and the affiliates. . . . As countries are going through the Arab Spring that will, territorially, present a substantial threat down the road." Asked if AQ was dead, Mueller responded in one word: "No."

Bruce Hoffman most recently defends an agnostic but deeply concerned perspective ("Al Qaeda's Uncertain Future," *Studies in Conflict & Terrorism*, 2013, Vol. 36, pp. 635-653). In opposition to "a recent State Department analysis" that AQ is "on a path of decline that will be difficult to reverse" and that this "general assessment also reflects the views of many prominent American pundits, academicians, and analysts," Hoffman argues for:

> a more cautious, even agnostic, approach. Although one cannot deny the vast inroads made against Core Al-Qaeda in recent years as a result of the developments described above, this article nonetheless argues that the long-established nucleus of the Al-Qaeda organization has proven itself to be as resilient as it is formidable. For more than a decade, it has withstood arguably the greatest international onslaught directed against a terrorist organization in history.

Further, it has consistently shown itself capable of adapting and adjusting to even the most consequential countermeasures directed against it, having, despite all odds, survived for nearly a quarter century.[636]

Further (p. 641):

the Al Qaeda Core's demise is neither ordained nor imminent—at least based on the publicly available evidence. Rather, one can make a reasonable argument that Core Al Qaeda has . . . well-established sanctuary in Pakistan . . . a deeper bench than has often been posited . . . a defined and articulated strategy for the future it is presumably still pursuing . . . a highly capable leader in al-Zawahiri . . . [and] . . . a well-honed, long established dexterity that enables it to be as opportunistic as it has been instrumental, that is capable of identifying and exploiting whatever new opportunities for expansion and consolidation may present themselves.

After citing numerous trends and concluding ,"[n]one of the above is pre-ordained, much less certain," Hoffman argues for another potential negative trajectory: "It is equally likely," he states (p. 648):

that Core Al Qaeda will continue to degenerate and eventually devolve into nothing more than a postmodern movement, with a set of loose ideas and ideologies. It would continue to pose a terrorist threat, but a far weaker, more sporadic and perhaps less consequential one. The future of the Al Qaeda Core depends not only on whether they can find a new cause—such as Syria today, like Iraq in 2003—but also, fundamentally, whether they can learn from past experiences and avoid the mistakes that previously undermined their struggle through self-inflicted wounds.

Powerful as Hoffman's argument is, and despite its solidity as an analysis of potential variables and drivers, this piece continues, mostly implicitly, an ongoing polemic with Marc Sageman over Sageman's thesis of the "leaderless jihad" and "bunch of guys" theory of emergent self-radicalization (see for example, p. 638; note 20; p. 649; p. 646) which likely explains the fact that Hoffman does not discuss the emergence of radicalization, self-radicalization, propaganda, counterpropaganda, or the present USG drone policy. Recent high-level intelligence community assessments view emergent cyberspace-based threats (internet-related attacks, espionage, and theft) as eclipsing the threat of an AQ-based mass casualty terrorist attack on U.S. soil; however, AQ-based, affiliated, and inspired terrorist attacks are still viewed as presenting major, persistent, highly complex, and varied threats across a variety of regions, including the American homeland. See for example: Greg Miller, "FBI director warns of cyberattacks; other security chiefs say terrorism threat has altered," *The Washington Post*, November 14, 2013, available from *www.washingtonpost.com/world/national-security*; Timothy M. Phelps, "Officials say terrorist threat on U.S. soil is declining," *Los Angeles Times*, November 14, 2013, available from *www.latimes.com/world/worldnow*. See also U.S. Department of State, "Country Reports on Terrorism," Fact Sheet, Washington DC: Office of the Spokesperson, May 30, 2013, available from *www.state.gov/r/pa/prs/ps/2013/05/210103.htm*, for further discussion of the consequences of attrition on AQ's centralized leadership and the emergence of geographically dispersed, decentralized, and relatively autonomous AQ-related terrorist acts from January 1, 2012, to December 31, 2012.

8. Consider, for example, the following telling contrast between former (1997-2005) Federal Bureau of Investigation (FBI) special agent Ali H. Soufan, who interrogated AQ detainees at the U.S. Naval Base in Guantanamo, Cuba (GITMO), and elsewhere; and Richard C. Clarke, former deputy national security advisor for counterterrorism. See Ali H. Soufan, "The End of the Jihadist Dream," *New York Times*, op-ed, May 3, 2011, p. A19:

> [I]t won't take long for Al Qaeda to begin wishing that Bin Laden wasn't dead. He not only was the embodiment of Al Qaeda's ideology, but also was central to the group's fundraising and recruiting successes. Without him, Al Qaeda will find itself short on cash—and members. . . . [N]o one in the organization can come close to filling that void. Bin Laden's deputy, Ayman al-Zawahiri, who will probably try to take over, is a divisive figure. His personality and leadership style alienate many, he lacks Bin Laden's charisma and connections and his Egyptian nationality is a major mark against him.

Richard C. Clarke, "Bin Laden's Dead. Al Qaeda's Not," *New York Times*, op-ed, May 3, 2011, p. A19, in stark contrast, asserts:

[E]ven before Bin Laden's death, analysts had begun to argue that Al Qaeda was rapidly becoming irrelevant. With Bin Laden's death, it is even more tempting to think that the era of Al Qaeda is over. But such rejoicing would be premature. To many Islamists ideologues, the Arab Spring simply represents the removal of obstacles that stood in the way of establishing the caliphate. Their goal has not changed, nor has their willingness to use terrorism. . . . The more significant threat . . . will come from Al Qaeda's local affiliates. Bin Laden and his deputies designed Al Qaeda as a network of affiliated groups that could operate largely independently to attack America, Europe and secular governments in the Middle East in order to establish fundamentalist regimes. Once in place, the network no longer needed Bin Laden and, in fact, has been proceeding with minimal direction from him for several years. . . . Islamist extremists will not be stopped by the elimination of Al Qaeda's leader or even by the eradication of Al Qaeda itself. They will continue their struggle, refusing to renounce violence or accept more democratic, less corrupt regimes as a substitute for the caliphate.

For commentary following bin Laden's death evidencing this divide, see for example, those asserting inevitable or likely post-bin Laden demise, Fouad Ajami, "Osama Bin Laden, Weak Horse," *The Wall Street Journal*, op-ed, May 3, 2001, available from *online. wsj.com*; Camille Tawil, "Bin Laden's death deals severe blow to al-Qaeda," March 5, 2011, available from *www.magharebia.com*, or post-bin Laden resilience, e.g., Eric Schmitt, "Ex-Counterterrorism Aide Warns Against Complacency on Al Qaeda," *The New York Times*, July 28, 2011; Tabassum Zakaria, "U.S. attack still significant al Qaeda goal: official," *Reuters*, July 26, 2011, available from *www.reuters.com*.

9. For select press on the embassy closings and worldwide travel alert, see Josh Hicks, "Chambliss: Threats 'very reminiscent of what we saw pre-9/11'," *The Washington Post*, August 4, 2013; Ahmed al-Haj and Krain Laub, "Tighter security at some US missions over al-Qaida," Associated Press, August 4, 2013; Martha Raddatz and Jonathan Karl, "Senior U.S. Official: Intercepted Al Qaeda Communications Indicate Planned Attack 'Big,' 'Strategically Significant'," ABC News, August 4, 2013; Thomas Joscelyn, "US Closes Diplomatic Facilities in Response to al Qaeda Threat,"

Long War Journal, 2013; Press, "US Embassies in 4 African Countries Also Closed," *The New York Times,* August 5, 2013, available from *www.nytimes.com/aponline/2013/08/05*; "US Orders Evacuation of Embassy in Yemen," VOA News, August 6, 2013, available from *www.voanews.com/articleprintview/1724146.html*; Eric Schmitt and Mark Mazzetti, "Qaeda Leader's Edict to Yemen Affiliate Is Said to Prompt Alert," *The New York Times*, August 6, 2013, available from *www.nytimes.com/2013/08/06*; Ellen Nakashima and Anne Gearan, "Al-Qaeda leader Zawahiri is said to have ordered terrorist attack; U.S. citizens urged to leave Yemen," *The Washington Post*, August 5, 2013, available from *www.washingtonpost. com*; Mohammed Ghobari, "U.S. citizens in Yemen urged to leave immediately," *Chicago Tribune*, August 6, 2013, available from *www.chicagotribune.com*. For commentary over whether the embassy closures evidenced an overreaction of the USG, especially in relation to fears resulting from the political fallout of the earlier Libyan embassy attack in Benghazi or a genuinely resilient and adaptive enemy, see Oren Dorell, "Al-Qaeda on the run? No way, say experts," *USA Today*, August 6, 2013, available from *www.usatoday.com*; Lara Jakes, "As al-Qaida grows, leaders remain a global threat," Associated Press, August 8, 2013, available from *www.sfgate.com*, "Far from being on the brink of collapse, al-Qaida's core leadership remains a potent threat—and one that experts say has encouraged he error network's spread into more countries today than it was operating in immediately after 9/11"; Marc A. Thiessen, "'Core al-Qaeda' is not defeated," *The Washington Post*, August 7, 2013, available from *www.washingtonpost.com/ opinions*; "UN Experts Say Al-Qaida Affiliates Remain a Threat," Associated Press, August 7, 2013, available from *www.nytimes. com*; Ken Dilanian, "Al Qaeda in the Arabian Peninsula at center of U.S. cross hairs," *Los Angeles Times*, August 7, 2013, available from *www.latimes.com*; Carla Babb, "US Concerned about Al-Qaida's Yemen Branch," VOA News, August 7, 2013, available from *www.voanews.com*; Jeffrey Goldberg, "Warning to Americans: Be Afraid, Very Afraid," August 4, 2013, available from *www. bloomberg.com*; Clint Watts, "Al Qaeda Plots, NSA Intercepts & the Era of Terrorism Competition," Philadelphia, PA: Foreign Policy Research Institute (FPRI), August 5, 2013, available from *www. fpri.org/print/1766*; BBC News, Middle East, "International press blame US for embassy closures," August 5, 2013, available from *www.bbc.co.uk*; Eugene Robinson, "The al-Qaeda menace the U.S. helped to create," *The Washington Post*, August 5, 2013, available from *www.washingtonpost.com/opinions*; The Editorial Board, "Terrorism and the Embassies," *The New York Times*, August 5, 2013, available from *www.nytimes.com/2013/08/06/opinion*; Juan Zarate and Thomas Sanderson, "Terrorism's shifting face," *The Washington Post*, August 5, 2013, available from *www.washingtonpost.com/opinions*; Editorial Board, "Wishful thinking on the war on terror," *The Washington Post*, August 5, 2013, available from *www.washingtonpost.com/opinions*; Dan Robinson, "White House Defends Progress Against al-Qaida, Affiliates," Voice of America, August 5, 2013, available from *www.voanews.com/articleprintview/1723104.html*; Kent Klein, "Obama: Al-Qaida Core 'On Its Way to Defeat'," VOA News, August 7, 2013, available from *www.voanews.com*.

10. National Consortium for the Study of Terrorism and Responses to Terrorism (START), "New data reveals AQ-linked groups among most active terrorist groups in the world," College Park, MD, University of Maryland, October 16, 2012, available at *www.start.umd.edu/news/new-data-reveals-al-qaida-linked-groups-among-most-active-terrorist-groups-world*. It should be noted that this START data combines data across groups that considerably differ in degree of formal subordination and global ambition. Some of these groups should be viewed as predominantly local or regional terrorist actors with more tenuous tactical cooperation but no formal subordination through an oath of loyalty to AQ emir Ayman al-Zawahiri or formal strategic alignment (e.g., Taliban, Boko Haram, Tehrik-i-Taliban Pakistan, and the Abu Sayyaf Group), whereas others are much more strategically aligned and formally subordinate (al-Qaeda in the Arabian Peninsula [AQAP]; al-Qaeda in the Islamic Magreb [AQIM]; Islamic State of Iraq [ISI]; Haqqani Network; al-Shabaab). Further, this data precedes the rise of additional affiliates and associates during the Arab Spring including major local, regional, and globalist actors in Northern and Western Africa, Syria, and the Sinai Peninsula.

11. START, "Annex of Statistical Information," Country Reports on Terrorism 2012, May 2013, available from *www.state.gov/documents/organization/210288.pdf*. This 2012 worldwide terrorist incident data further corroborates the role of more loosely-aligned affiliates and predominantly regional Islamist insurgent terrorist organizations. For example, of these six organizations, the Afghanistan-based Taliban and Boko Haram alone are responsible for 889 terrorist acts and 2,974 deaths, together account-

ing for 60 percent of terrorist attacks and 60 percent of deaths. For a brief account of the diversified nature of the present threat posed by these regional actors, see also U.S. Department of State, *Country Reports on Terrorism Fact Sheet*, Washington DC: Office of the Spokesperson, May 2013, available from *www.state.gov/r/pa/prs/ps/2013/05/210103.htm*. For the full report, see United States Department of State, *Country Reports on Terrorism*, Washington, DC: Bureau of Counterterrorism, May 2013, available from *www.state.gov/documents/organization/210204.pdf*.

12. See for example, Adam Goldman, "Terrorists turn to online chat rooms to evade U.S.," *Japan Times*, August 15, 2013, available from *www.legalnews.com/detroit/1379327*. Thomas Joscelyn, "CNN on al Qaeda's 'encrypted messaging system'," *Long War Journal*, August 9, 2013, available from *www.longwarjournal.org*; Thomas Joscelyn and Bill Roggio, "Analysis: Recent embassy closures triggered by Zawahiri communications with multiple subordinates," *Long War Journal*, August 9, 2013, available from *www.longwarjournal.org*; Barbara Starr, "Details emerge about talk between al Qaeda leaders," August 9, 2013, available from *security.blogs.cnn.com/2013/08/09*; Paul Cruickshank and Tim Lister, "Al Qaeda calling?" August 8, 2013, available from *security.blogs.cnn.com/2013/08/08*. See also Yotam Rosner, Aviad Mendelbaum, Sean London, and Yoram Schweitzer, "Backdoor Plots: The Darknet as a Field for Terrorism," *INSS Insight* No. 464, September 10, 2013, available from *www.inss.org.il*. Recent reporting suggests, however, that the U.S. intelligence community, particularly the National Security Agency, have developed an astonishingly powerful array of techniques for infiltrating and exploiting AQ's communications networks (see for example, Greg Miller, Julie Tate, and Barton Gellman, "Documents reveal NSA's extensive involvement in targeted killing program," *The Washington Post*, October 16, 2013, available from *www.washingtonpost.com/world/national-security*.

13. Office of the President of the United States, *Empowering Local Partners to Prevent Violent Extremism in the United* States, Washington, DC: The White House, August 3, 2013, pp. 1-2; Department of Homeland Security, *Quadrennial Homeland Security Review Report: A Strategic Framework for a Secure Homeland*, Washington, DC: Department of Homeland Security, February 2010, pp. 21-23, available from *www.dhs.gov/xlibrary/assets/qhsr_report.pdf*; U.S. Department of Homeland Security, *Department of Home-*

land Security Strategic Plan, Fiscal Years 2012-2016, Washington, DC: Department of Homeland Security, February 2012, pp. 3-4, available from *www.dhs.gov/strategic-plan-fiscal-years-fy-2012-2016*; Office of the President of the United States, *National Strategy for Counterterrorism*, Washington, DC: The White House, June 2011, pp. 1-4; The Honorable Matthew G. Olsen, Director, National Counterterrorism Center, "Hearing before the House Committee on Homeland Security, Understanding the Threat Landscape, Washington, DC: U.S. House of Representatives, July 25, 2012, esp. pp. 1-4; James R. Clapper, Director of National Intelligence, *Statement for the Record, Worldwide Threat Assessment of the US Intelligence Community*, Washington, DC: House Permanent Select Committee on Intelligence, April 11, 2013, pp. 3-5; Obama, "The Future of our Fight Against Terrorism."

14. National Commission on Terrorist Attacks Upon the United States, *Final Report of the National Commission on Terrorist Attacks Upon the United States* (aka: *The 9/11 Commission Report*), New York: W. W. Norton, 2004, Chap. 12, "What to do? A Global Strategy," pp. 361-398.

15. See *9/11 Commission Report*, pp. 365-374.

16. The Honorable Matthew G. Olsen, Director, National Counterterrorism Center, "Hearing before the House Committee on Homeland Security, Understanding the Threat Landscape," Washington, DC: U.S. House of Representatives, July 25, 2012, esp. pp. 1-4.

17. Clapper, *Statement for the Record, Worldwide Threat Assessment of the US Intelligence Community*, pp. 3-5.

18. Obama, "The Future of our Fight Against Terrorism."

19. Select examples of high value detainees include Khalid Sheikh Mohammad (KSM), captured March 2003 in Pakistan; incarcerated in GITMO; Abu Faraj al Libi, captured May 2005, incarcerated in GITMO; Ramzi Bin al-Shihb, captured September 2002, incarcerated in GITMO; Umar Patek, the 2002 Bali nightclub bomber mastermind, captured by Pakistani forces, January 2011; Younis al-Mauritani, captured by Pakistani forces, September 2011; Hambali (aka: Riduan Isamuddin), captured in a joint U.S.-

Thai operation in Thailand, August 2003; al Rahim al Nashiri, the head of AQ in the Persian Gulf, and mastermind of USS *Cole* bombing, captured November 2002, incarcerated in GITMO; Ali al Aziz Ali KSM's nephew and chief deputy, captured in 2003, incarcerated in GITMO; Walid bin Attash, captured March 2003, incarcerated in GITMO; and Nazih Abdul Hamed al Ruqai (aka: Abu Anas al-Libi), under indictment on October 5, 2013, for the 1998 East African embassy bombings, and, since shortly after 9/11, wanted by the FBI with a $5 million dollar bounty offered for his capture. See Thomas Joscelyn, "'Core' al Qaeda member captured in Libya," *Long War Journal*, 2013, available from *www. longwarjournal.org/archives/2013/10/core_al_qaeda_member.php*. For the hybrid legal process involving both the military and civilian justice systems, i.e., preserving the opportunity and right to rendition and interrogation under military jurisdiction of al-Libi for the purposes of intelligence collection, but also under conditions that ensures due process in a U.S. federal district court, see "Obama Praises Capture of African Embassies Bombing Suspect," VOA News, October 8, 2013; Benjamin Weiser and Eric Schmitt, "U.S. Said to Hold Qaeda Suspect on Navy Ship," *The New York Times*, October 6, 2013; Charlie Savage and Benjamin Weiser, "How the U.S. Is Interrogating a Qaeda Suspect," *The New York Times*, October 7, 2013; Ernesto Londono, "Capture of bombing suspect in Libya represents rare 'rendition' by U.S. military," *The Washington Post*, October 6, 2013, available from *www.washington-post.com/world/national-security*; Ken Dilanian and David S. Cloud, "U.S. raids on Al Qaeda operatives show shift away from drone strikes," *Los Angeles Times*, October 6, 2013, available from *www. latimes.com/world*; Benjamin Weiser, "Captured in Libya, 1998 Bombing Suspect Pleads Not Guilty in a Manhattan Court," *The New York Times*, October 15, 2013.

20. Obama, "The Future of our Fight Against Terrorism."

21. The present discussion is limited to presenting these data in support of the thesis of efficaciousness. Other key variables, feasibility and acceptability/perceived legitimacy are not directly addressed, but will be discussed as appropriate when considering strategic recommendations. For the rationale supporting the hunting of leadership targets in terrorist organizations, see Graham H. Turbiville, Jr., *Hunting Leadership Targets in Counterinsurgency and Counterterrorist Operations: Selected Perspectives and Experience*,

JSOU Report 07-6, Hurlburt Field, FL, The JSOU Press, June 2007, available from *jsoupublic.socom.mil*; George A. Crawford, *Manhunting: Counter-Network Organization in Irregular Warfare*, JSOU Report 09-7, Hurlburt Field, FL, September 2009, available from *jsoupublic.socom.mil*. For the origin of the covert drone program in Pakistan, see Brian Glyn Williams, "The CIA's Covert Predator Drone War in Pakistan, 2004-2010: The History of an Assassination Campaign," *Studies in Conflict and Terrorism*, Vol. 33, 2010, pp. 871-892; Mark Mazzetti, "A Secret Deal on Drones, Sealed in Blood," *The New York Times*, April 6, 2013, available from *www.nytimes.com*; Jonathan S. Landay, "CIA collaborated with Pakistan spy agency in drone war," *Stars and Stripes*, April 9, 2013, available from *www.stripes.com*; Greg Miller and Bob Woodward, "Secret memos reveal explicit nature of U.S., Pakistan agreement on drones," *The Washington Post*, October 24, 2013, available from *www.washingtonpost.com/world/national-security*; "Secret memos 'show Pakistan endorsed drone strikes'," BBC News, October 24, 2013, available from *nationaluasi.com/dru/secret-memos-show-sakistan-endorsed-us-drone-strikes-102413*. For the drones as official USG policy, see Micah Zenko, "The Long Third War: No matter who wins in November, America should get ready for 10 more years of drones," *Foreign Policy*, October 30, 2012, available from *www.foreignpolicy.com*; Peter Bergen and Katherine Tiedemann, "Washington's Phantom War: The Effects of the U.S. Drone Program in Pakistan," *Foreign Affairs*, July/August 2011, Vol. 90, No. 4, pp. 12-18; Jo Becker and Scott Shane, "Secret 'Kill List' Proves a Test of Obama's Principles and Will," *The New York Times*, May 29, 2012, available from *www.nytimes.com*; Mark Mazzetti, , "The Drone Zone," *The New York Times*, July 6, 2012, available from *www.nytimes.com*; David Ignatius, "An embassy asks, Drones or diplomacy?" *The Washington Post* op-ed, June 20, 2012, available from *www.washingtonpost.com*; Luis Ramirez, "Drones Revolutionize US Warfare," VOA News, June 9, 2012, available from *www.voanews.com*; Scott Shane, "Targeted Killing Comes to Define War on Terror," *The New York Times*, April 7, 2013, available from *www.nytimes.com*; Pat Reber, "Reports: US drone command to shift from CIA to military," *Stars and Stripes*, March 21, 2013, available from *www.stripes.com*; Ken Dilanian, "CIA's covert drone program might shift further to Pentagon," *Stars and Stripes*, February 17, 2013, available from *www.stripes.com*; Gordon Lubold and Shane Harris, "Exclusive: The CIA, Not the Pentagon, Will Keep Running Obama's Drone War," *Foreign Policy*, November 7,

2013, available from *droneswatch.org/2013/11/06/exclusive-the-cia-not-the-pentagon-will-keep-running-obamas-drone-war/*. Greg Miller, "CIA remains behind most drone strikes, despite effort to shift campaign to Defense," *The Washington Post*, November 25, 2013, available from *www.washingtonpost.com/world/national-security/*; *Reuters*, "Kerry Says Obama Has Timeline to End U.S. Drone Strikes in Pakistan," *The New York Times*, August 1, 2013; Cora Currier, "6 Months After Obama Promise to Divulge More on Drones, Here's What We Still Don't Know," November, 5, 2013.

Some assert that, while undeniably successful as a tactic, drones may be self-defeating as strategy since it is deemed morally outrageous and unacceptable by many and may serve instead to replenish ranks even faster due to radicalization and recruitment (see e.g., Arie Kruglanski and Anna C. Sheveland, "Paradoxes of Counterterrorism," November 27, 2012, available from *nationalinterest.org*). These authors state: "[T]he most effective tactical tool in the fight against terrorism turns out to be a major hindrance to U.S. strategic objectives, causing Washington to be hoist by its own petard." See Audrey Kurth Cronin, "Why Drones Fail: When Tactics Drive Strategy," *Foreign Affairs*, Vol. 92, No. 4, July/August 2013, pp. 44-54. Others assert that the drone policy does, in fact, contribute to sound strategy, and that its costs, while undeniable, do not outweigh its benefits. For a defense of the present policy, see Daniel Byman, "Why Drones Work: The Case for Washington's Weapon of Choice," *Foreign Affairs*, Vol. 92, No. 4, July/August 2013, pp. 32-43; Carla Babb, "Drone Strikes Key as Terror Threat Keeps US Embassies Closed," VOA News, August 7, 2013, available from *www.voanews.com*; Patrick B. Johnson, "Drone Strikes Keep Pressure on al-Qaida," Santa Monica, CA: The RAND Corporation, August 18, 2012, available from *www.rand.org/commentary/2012/08/18/PJ.html*; Mark Hosenball, "Scaled-back Pakistan drone strikes reflect success: U.S. official," *Reuters*, April 13, 2013, available from *www.reuters.com*; Dr. W. Andrew Terrill, (Op-Ed: Drones are Making a Difference in Yemen," March 13, 2013, available from *www.strategicstudies inistitute.army.mil*) states: "At least in the case of Yemen, drones appear to have been stunningly successful in achieving goals that support the U.S. and Yemeni national interests by helping to defeat the radical group al-Qaeda in the Arabian Peninsula." Michael W. Lewis, "The case for drone strikes: they remain the best option for denying Al Qaeda and Taliban fighters havens in Pakistan," op-ed, *Los Angeles Times*, February 5, 2013, available from *articles.latimes.com/2013/feb/05/opinion/la-oe-lewis-defending-drones-20130205;* Michael W. Lewis, "Drones: Actually the Most Humane Form of Warfare Ever," *The Atlantic,* August 21, 2013; Mark Bowden, "The Killing Machines: How to Think about Drones," *The Atlantic,* September 2013; George Will, "A case for targeted killings," *The Washington Post,* op-ed, December 7, 2012, available from *www.washingtonpost.com;* Mark R. Jacobson, "Five myths about Obama's drone war," *The Washington Post,* February 8, 2013, available from *www.washingtonpost.com;* Shehzad H. Qazi, "Four Myths about Drone Strikes," *The Diplomat,* June 9, 2012, available from *the-diplomat.com.* See also James Igoe Walsh, *The Effectiveness of Drone Strikes in Counterinsurgency and Counterterrorism Campaigns,* Carlisle, PA: Strategic Studies Institute, U.S. Army War College, September 2013, for a measured, strategically nuanced, regionally specific analysis which, among other findings, recommends that drones be considered merely one tactic embodied in broader policies addressing the phenomenon of failing and failed states, the complexity of intra-insurgent alliances, and the actual evidence associating the use of drones with declining insurgent violence. Finally, recent emphases by the Afghan Taliban and AQAP on USG drone policy is telling, since, at the very least, effort is expended attempting to delegitimize and undermine support for their use. See for example, Bill Roggio, "Afghan Taliban say drone strikes are proof the US is a 'paper tiger'," *Long War Journal,* December 9, 2013, available from *www.longwarjournal.org/archives/2013/12;* Hunzala, "Report: A reflection on the American Drone War Strategy," *Shahamat,* November 25, 2013, available from *shahamat-english.com/index.php/articles;* Bill Roggio, "AQAP says assault on Yemen's Defense Ministry targeted US drone operations," *Long War Journal,* December 6, 2013, available from *www.longwarjournal.org.*

Consider also the contrasting positions over whether genuine widespread opposition to this policy exists and is substantial enough to call the policy into question. See e.g., Sharon Behn, "Study: US Should Re-Evaluate Pakistan Drone Strikes," VOA News, September 26, 2012, available from *www.voanews.com;* Reuters, "Obama Victory Infuriates Pakistani Drone Victims," *The New York Times,* November 8, 2012, available from *www.nytimes. com;* Toshio Suzuki, "Study shows widespread global opposition to US drone strikes," *Stars and Stripes,* June 13, 2012, available from *www.stripes.com;* Henry Ridgwell, "US Drone Strikes Under Scrutiny," VOA News, April 9, 2013, available from *www.*

voanews.com; Nic Robertson, "In Swat Valley, U.S. drone strikes radicalizing a new generation," CNN News, April 15, 2013, available from *www.cnn.com/2013/04/14/world/asia/pakistan-swat-valley-school/index.html*; *Reuters*, "Obama Victory Infuriates Pakistani Drone Victims," *The New York Times*, November 8, 2012, available from *www.nytimes.com*; Toshio Suzuki, "Study shows widespread global opposition to US drone strikes," *Stars and Stripes*, June 13 2012, available from *www.stripes.com*. Or, to the contrary, that in general opposition to drones is highly variable and, in fact, mostly muted, assuming unintended civilian noncombatant deaths are kept to the barest minimum, among those most directly victimized by AQ and its allies and affiliates. See e.g., Greg Miller, "In interview, Yemeni president acknowledges approving U.S. drone strikes," *The Washington Post*, September 29, 2012, available from *www.washingtonpost.com*; C. Christine Fair, Karl C. Kaltenthaler and William J. Miller, "You Say Pakistanis All hate the Drone War? Prove It," *The Atlantic*, January 2013, available from *www. theatlantic.com*; Hasnain Kazim, "Pakistani CIA Informant: 'Drone Attacks are the Right Thing to Do'," *Spiegel*, December 4, 2013, available from *www.spiegel.de/international/zeitgeist*.

22. See Department of Justice White Paper, "Lawfulness of a Lethal Operation Directed Against a U.S. Citizen Who Is a Senior Operational Leader of Al-Qa'ida or An Associated Force," February 4, 2013, available from *msnbcmedia.msn.com/i/msnbc/sections/news/020413_DOJ_White_Paper.pdf*, for the lawfulness under U.S. and international law of targeting an American national who has joined AQ or its associated forces. The following legal findings are key: a lethal operation in a foreign nation would be consistent with international legal principles of sovereignty and neutrality if it were conducted, for example, with the consent of the host nation's government or after a determination that the host nation is unable or unwilling to suppress the threat posed by the individual targeted pp. 1-2. "The United States is currently in a non-international armed conflict with al-Qa'ida and its associated forces (See *Hamdan v. Rumsfeld*, 548 U.S. 557, 628-31, 2006), holding that a conflict between a nation and a transnational nonstate actor occurring outside the nation's territory is an armed conflict 'not of an international character' (quoting Common Article 3 of the Geneva Conventions) because it is not a 'clash between nations' (p. 3). The primary basis for authority exists in inherent Presidential authority, the constitutional responsibility to protect

the country, the inherent right of the United States to national self-defense under international law, Congress's authorization of the use of all necessary and appropriate military force against this enemy, and the existence of an armed conflict with al-Qa'ida under international law are legal grounds for using force against an American citizen who is a senior operational leader of al Qa'ida or an associated force. Where an associated force as defined in footnote 1 refers to a "co-belligerent" under the laws of war are met, specifically, (1) an informed high-level official of the U.S. Government has determined that the targeted individual poses an imminent threat of violent attack against the United States; (2) capture is infeasible, and the United States continues to monitor whether capture becomes feasible; and (3) the operation would be conducted in a manner consistent with applicable law of war principles (p. 1, 6). Additionally, the fact that "such an operation would not violate certain criminal provisions prohibiting the killing of U.S. nationals outside the United States; nor would it constitute either a commission of a war crime or an assassination prohibited by Executive Order 12333" (p. 2); that "the four fundamental law-of-war principles governing the use of force: necessity, distinction, proportionality, and humanity (the avoidance of unnecessary suffering)" are observed (p. 8). Finally, that this does not "violate the prohibitions against treachery and perfidy, which address a breach of confidence by the assailant" (p. 8). See also John Yoo, "Assassination or Targeted Killings after 9/11," 56 *N.Y. L. Sch. L. Rev.* 57 (2011), available from *scholarship.law.berkely.edu/facpubs/1215,* for an excellent discussion of policy; legality (especially the distinction between political assassination in peacetime versus targeted killing and its limits in wartime); its legality in constitutional, congressional, and statutory law, and the laws of war; and finally, its soundness as a tactic in an asymmetric war with an AQ terrorist enemy organized as a decentralized free-scale terrorist network parasitizing the Western legal and social order. See also David G. Savage, "Obama adviser who decried 'war on terror' now defends drones," *Stars and Stripes*, January 5, 2013, available from *www.stripes.com.* This describes Harold Hongju Koh's (dean of Yale and State Department's legal adviser in first Obama administration) acceptance and defense of the current policy. See also James Jay Carafano, "Say What You Want About Drones—They're Perfectly Legal," *The Atlantic*, August 2013, available from *www.theatlantic.com/international/archive/2013/08/say-what-you-want-about-drones-theyre-perfectly-legal/278740/.*

23. See for example, Michael R. Gordon and Eric Schmitt, "U.S. Officials Propose Sharing Drone Surveillance Data with Algerians," *The New York Times*, February 26, 2013, available from *www.nytimes.com*; Tara Kelly, "France 'to buy US drones'," July 4, 2013, available from *www.france24.com*; Mark Mazzetti, "C.I.A. Building Base for Strikes in Yemen," *The New York Times*, June 14, 2011, available from *www.nytimes.com*; *Reuters*, "Yemen Asks US for Drones to Fight Al-Qaida," VOA News, August 22, 2013, available from *www.voanews.com/1735074.html*; Bill Roggio, "US Reapers flying from Ethiopia," *Long War Journal*, October 27, 2011, available from *www.longwarjournal.org*; Craig Whitlock, "U.S. troops arrive in Niger to set up drone base," *The Washington Post*, February 22, 2013, available from *www.washingtonpost.com*; Craig Whitlock, "Drone base in Niger gives U.S. a strategic foothold in West Africa," *The Washington Post* March 21, 2013, available from *www.washingtonpost.com*; VOA News, "Report: US Building Drone Bases in Africa, Arabian Peninsula," September 21, 2011, available from *www.voanews.com*; Greg Miller, "Secret drone bases: Avoiding past mistakes," *The Washington Post*, September 21, 2011, available from *www.washingtonpost.com/blogs*.

24. The recent use of conditional language by Secretary of State John Kerry regarding the USG drone policy in Pakistan is telling. Asked when the drone program will end, Secretary Kerry replies: "I **think** the program will end as we have eliminated **most** of the threat and continue to eliminate it. . . . The president has a very real timeline, and we **hope** it's going to be very, very **soon**." (emphasis added). See also Mark Mazzetti and Mark Landler, "Despite Administration Promises, Few Signs of Change in Drone Wars," *The New York Times*, August 2, 2013, available from *www.nytimes.com*. Also, despite some press reports indicating a major shift in drone policy (e.g., Charlie Savage and Peter Baker, "Obama, in a Shift, to Limit Targets of Drone Strikes," *The New York Times*, May 22, 2013, available from *www.nytimes.com*; Michael O'Hanlon, "Obama Speech Nails It On Drone Strikes," May 24, 2013, available from *www.realclearpolitics.com/articles/2013/05/24/obama_speech_nails_it_on_drone_strikes_118541.html*. Peter Baker, "Pivoting from a War Footing, Obama Acts to Curtail Drones," *The New York Times*, May 23, 2013, available from *www.nytimes.com*), others discern that a careful defense and rationale were outlined in the President's major foreign policy speech

delivered at the National Defense University, Washington, DC, on May 23, 2013, that focused on suitability and moral legitimacy, and **not** a proposed reduction or demotion of its role in combating the AQ terrorist entity (e.g., BBC News, U.S. and Canada, "Barack Obama defends 'just war' using drones," May 24, 2013, available from *www.bbc.co.uk*; Mark Mazzetti, "Analysis of Key Points from Obama's Speech on Drones," May 23, 2013, available from *thecaucus.blogs.nytimes.com*).

25. Bill Roggio and Alexander Mayer, "Charting the data for US airstrikes in Pakistan, 2004-2013," *Long War Journal*, November 29, 2013.

26. New America Foundation, "The Drone War in Pakistan," November 21, 2013, available from *natsec.newamerica.net/drones/pakistan/analysis*.

27. Bill Roggio and Alexander Mayer, "Senior al Qaeda and Taliban leaders killed in US airstrikes in Pakistan, 2004-2013," *Long War Journal*, November 23, 2013, available from *www.longwarjournal.org/pakistan-strikes-hvts.php*.

28. At the time of his death on June 4, 2012, Yahya al-Libi was one of AQ's most formidable figures. (See Bill Roggio, "Abu Yahya al Libi killed in latest drone strike, US officials say," *Long War Journal*, June 5, 2012, available from *www.longwarjournal.org/archives/2012/06/abu_yahya_al_libi_ru.php*). He had become, Roggio states, "one of al Qaeda's most prolific propagandists" and between 2006-10 had "appeared in more AQ propaganda tapes than any other member of the terror group, including bin Laden and Zawahiri" and had "stepped into the role of chief of staff for Ayman al Zawahiri after Osama bin Laden was killed by U.S. special operations forces in Abbottabad, Pakistan, in May 2011." Having been "deputy to Atiyah abd al Rahman," al-Libi was "elevated to second in command after Atiyah's death in a drone strike."

29. Roggio and Mayer, "Senior al Qaeda and Taliban leaders killed in US airstrikes in Pakistan, 2004-2013."

30. Thomas Joscelyn and Bill Roggio, "AQAP's emir also serves as al Qaeda's general manager," *Long War Journal*, August 6, 2013.

31. Bill Roggio and Bob Barry, "Charting the data for US air strikes in Yemen, 2002-2013," *Long War Journal*, December 9, 2013, available from *www.longwarjournal/org/multimedia/Yemen/ code/Yemen-strike.php*. Interested readers should note that these figures are constantly updated, and this author is limited by the data available at the time of writing. Each day's headlines promise fresh data. For example, beyond the data reported above, one should add Al Khidr al Ja'dani (overall commander for AQAP in Abyan province, killed in a July 30, 2013, drone strike (see Bill Roggio, "Local AQAP commander reported killed in recent US drone strike," *Long War Journal*, August 3, 2013, available from *www.longwarjournal.org/archives/2013/08/local_aqap_commander-print.php*.) Also, such headlines as these recommends constant updating of overall casualty estimates:

> The US launched its third drone strike in Yemen in the past 5 days, killing five al Qaeda in the Arabian Peninsula operatives in an area of eastern Yemen that is said to be under control of the terrorist group. . . . No senior al Qaeda operatives or leaders are reported to have been killed at this time. The identities of the Al Qaeda operatives who were killed have not been disclosed. . . . Hadramount is the ancestral home of Osama bin Laden's family, and the province has become an AQAP bastion over the past several years.

See Bill Roggio, "US drones kill 5 AQAP operatives in Yemen," *Long War Journal*, August 1, 2013, available from *www.longwarjournal.org/archives/2013/08/us_drones_kill_5_aqa_1.php*.

32. According to press accounts (see Lara Kasinof, Mark Mazzetti, and Alan Cowell, "U.S.-Born Qaeda Leader Killed in Yemen," *The New York Times*, September 30, 2011. This this U.S. born Yemeni was "associated with many plots in the United States and elsewhere after individuals planning violence were drawn to his engaging lectures broadcast over the internet." Awlaki had "taken to the Internet with stirring battle cries directed at young Muslims," beseeching them by declaring "Many of your scholars are standing between you and your duty of jihad." Since December 2009, other top leaders of AQAP have been targeted — including Abu Basir al Wuhayshi, the group's leader; Abu Hurayrah Qasim al Ramyi, its military commander; and Ibrahim Sulei-

man al Rubaish, its top sharia official. Said Ali al Shihri, AQAP's deputy commander, died late-2012 due to drone-related injuries sustained November 28, 2012 (see Mark Mazzetti, "No. 2 Leader of Al Qaeda in Yemen is Killed," *The New York Times*, January 24, 2013.

33. Peter Bergen and David Sterman, "Falling under the spell of a slain terrorist," CNN News, June 28, 2013, available from *www.cnn.com/2013/06/28/opinion/bergen-awlaki-influence*. Bill Roggio, "Yemen claims cleric Anwar al Awlaki 'killed' in airstrike," *Long War Journal*, September 30, 2011, available from *www.longwarjournal.org/*. Roggio reports of Awlaki during 2010 and before his killing ("US-born cleric Awlaki 'proud' to have taught al Qaeda operatives," *Long War Journal*, April 27, 2010, available from *www.longwarjournal.org/archives/2010/04/usborn_cleric_awlaki-print.php*) that Awlaki was a spiritual advisor to 9/11 hijackers Nawaf al Hazmi and Khalid Almihdhar; that another 9/11 hijacker Hani Hanjour attended his sermons; and that Ramzi Binalshib, the primary intermediary between Osama bin Laden and 9/11 mastermind Khaled Sheikh Muhammad, had Awlaki's phone number discovered at his residence. According to Roggio:

> Awlaki has become a prominent cyber-jihadist. Combining his ability to communicate in English with his charisma with young, radical Muslims and his presence on the Web, Awlaki has developed a large following. He gives numerous lectures and speeches via the Internet and teleconferences. U.S. law enforcement agencies and intelligence services consider Awlaki to be a prime recruiter for al-Qaeda as well as a provider of the needed religious justifications, or fatwas, for jihadis to carry out attacks.

See also Alexander Meleagrou-Hitchens, "Anwar al-'Awlaqi's Disciples: Three Case Studies," *CT Sentinel*, Vol. 4, Issue 7, July 2011, pp. 6-9; Rajib and Tehzeeb Karim, February 2010 conviction for attempted attack on British Airways; Faisal Shahzad, May 2010 attempt to detonate a car bomb in New York City's Times Square; and "Terror plot shows cleric's reach," *USA Today*, November 22, 2011, available from *www.usatoday.com/*.

34. See Michael Muskal, "'Underwear bomber' pleads guilty in airline plot," *Los Angeles Times*, October 13, 2011, available

from *www.latimes.com*; Peter Finn, "Attempted bomber of Detroit-bound plane gets life in prison," *The Washington Post*, February 16, 2012, available from *www.washingtonpost.com*.

35. See Majority and Minority Staff, Senate Committee on Homeland and Security and Governmental Affairs, Washington, DC: U.S. Senate, *Zachary Chesser: A Case Study in Online Islamist Radicalization and Its Meaning for the Threat of Homegrown Terrorism*, February 2012; also see Tara Bahrampour, "Internet helped Muslim covert from Northern Virginia embrace extremism at warp speed," *The Washington Post*, November 2, 2010, available from *www.washingtonpost.com*.

36. James Dao, "Man Claims Terror Ties in Little Rock Shooting," *The New York Times*, January 22, 2010.

37. Bill Rogio and Lisa Sundquist, "European terror plot begins to unravel," *Long War Journal*, September 29, 2010, available from *www.longwarjournal.org*; Thomas Joscelyn and Bill Roggio, "Osama bin Laden ordered Mumbai-style attacks in Europe," *Long War Journal*, October 1, 2010, available from *www.longwarjournal.org*.

38. Eric Schmitt and Thom Shanker, "Qaeda Trying to Harness Toxin For Bombs, U.S. Officials Fear," *The New York Times*, August 12, 2011, available from *www.nytimes.com*, report on AQAP's attempt to concoct, deploy, and explode a ricin-based explosive. Ricin, derived from very large quantities of castor beans, is required "to produce ricin, a white, powdery toxin that is so deadly that just a speck can kill if it is inhaled or reaches the bloodstream." AQAP's specific goal is to "secretly concoct batches of the poison, pack them around small explosives, and then try to explode them in contained spaces, like a shopping mall, an airport, or a subway station."

39. Josh Meyer, "This Man Would Like to Turn Anyone's Clothes into a Bomb," *The Atlantic*, August 2013, available from *www.theatlantic.com*. This report profiles AQAP's Ibrahim Hassan al Asiri, the terror group's top bomb maker "who has designed devices that are said to be undetectable by traditional screening methods."

40. Bill Roggio, "Wuhayshi imparted lessons of AQAP operations in Yemen to AQIM," *The Long War Journal*, August 12, 2013, available from *www.longwarjournal.org*.

41. Killed October 1, 2012, while traveling in a vehicle in the Mir Ali area of North Waziristan, Ghul divulged the name of Osama bin Laden's key courier, Abu Ahmed al Kuwaiti, during coercive Central Intelligence Agency (CIA) -led interrogation. This was instrumental in ultimately locating the Abbottabad compound. Turned over to Pakistan in 2006, he was released 1 year later, and from that date, played a pivotal role in reestablishing AQ's Pakistani network. See Bill Roggio, "Senior al Qaeda leader and former US detainee killed in drone strike in 2012," October 17, 2013, available from *www.longwarjournal.org/archives/2013/10*.

42. Raheem Salman and Ned Parker, "The Great Escape: How al Qaeda broke hundreds of bad guys out of the world's most notorious jail—and what it means for America," *Foreign Policy*, August 5, 2013, available from *www.foreignpolicy.com*.

43. Mohammad Ghobari reports, for example ("U.S. citizens in Yemen urged to leave immediately," *Chicago Tribune*, August 6, 2013, available from *www.chicagotribune.com*), that 25 senior AQ militants are being sought by Yemeni security forces each with a 5 million Yemeni riyal ($23,000U.S.) bounty on each for information leading to their capture.

44. Ayman al-Zawahiri (see Adam Goldman and Kathy Gannon, Associated Press, "CIA has come close to getting bin Laden deputy," *Washington Times*, December 1, 2010, available from *www.washingtontimes.com*) has escaped several operations including a CIA attempted abduction in Pakistan in 2003, an attempted bombing in Pakistan in 2004, and a U.S. missile strike in 2006.

45. Sirajuddin Haqqani, operations commander of the Haqqani Network, apparently escaped a drone strike that killed three Haqqani commanders just 11 days after his brother Nasiruddin Haqanni, the group's main financier and son to the group's founder, Mawlawi Jalaluddin Haqqani, was killed in an unsolved drive-by shooting in Rawalpindi, Pakistan. See Bill Roggio, "US drone strike kills 3 Haqqani commanders in Pakistan's Hangu district," *Long War Journal*, November 21, 2013, available from

www.longwarjournal.org/archives/2013/11; BBC News, "Nasirud-din Haqqani: Senior militant shot dead in Pakistan," November 11, 2013.

46. See BBC, South Asia, "Al-Qaeda's remaining leaders," available from *www.bbc.co.uk/news/world-south-asia-11489337*; "Al-Qaida's most wanted," March 9, 2013, available from *news.msn. com/world/al-qaidas-most-wanted*; Bill Roggio, "US kills 4 AQAP operatives in Yemen drone strike," *Long War Journal*, August 6, 2013, available from *www.longwarjournal.org/archives/2013/08/us_kills_6_aqap_oper-print.php*.

47. Relative success for this third strategic objective arises from the USG identifying and emphasizing those variables over which it has a degree of control. Conducting a terrorist attack requires three key ingredients: ability, opportunity, and motive. Ability, i.e., what might be termed "terrorcraft," involves the acquisition of skills, capacities, and training. Opportunity requires access to finances, sanctuary, weaponry, communication, travel, and ultimately, targets. Least controllable and predictable is the realm of motives, grievances, and psychological drivers. George Quester, some years ago in the final semi-dissenting essay in a text focusing on motive and morality (see "Eliminating the Terrorist Opportunity," David C. Rapoport and Yonah Alexander, eds., *The Morality of Terrorism: Religious and Secular Justifications*, New York: Pergamon Press, 1982, pp. 325-346) provides the rationale for such a focus on controlling opportunity (p. 325):

> Some portions of the phenomenon of terrorism are clearly explained by the frustrations and injustices of our society and by the sociology or psychology of the individuals then driven to enlist in terrorist groups. Other portions of terrorist activity stem from technological or social changes which make terrorist attacks easier or harder.... [It is m]y contention that opportunity plays an underrated role here, while the values and grievances of the rebel have disproportionate attention.... [T]he working premise, regardless of whatever causes terrorism, is that opportunities provided by technological change are more manipulable and controllable than the plane of value preferences; it will be easier to lock up the boarding areas of airports than to change the feelings of the would-be skyjacker, or to attend to his grievances which are sometimes quite bizzare. Moreover, whatever the cur-

rent significance of personal motivation or physical opportunity in the explanation or control of terrorism, the trend
over time may have to be toward the control of opportunity,
as some very significant and dangerous avenues of attack
are opening by which the terrorists can make his mark on
society.

48. *The 9/11 Commission Report*, pp. 383-398.

49. See for example, U.S. Department of Homeland Security,
*Quadrennial Homeland Security Review Report: A Strategic Frame-
work for a Secure Homeland*, February 2010, available from *www.
dhs.gov/xlibrary/assets/qhsr_report.pdf*. This first-ever *Quadrennial
Homeland Security Review* (QHSR), pursuant to the *Implementing
Recommendations of the 9/11 Commission Act of 2007*, covers "threats
presented and the framework for our strategic response" (p. iii),
and covers five key missions: 1) Preventing Terrorism and Enhancing Security (three goals: prevent terrorist attacks; prevent
unauthorized use of Chemical, Biological. Radiological, Nuclear
(CBRN) materials and capabilities; manage risks to critical infrastructure, key leadership, and events); 2) Securing and Managing
Our Borders (three goals: effectively control U.S. air, land, and
sea borders; safeguard lawful trade and travel; disrupt and dismantle transnational criminal organizations); 3) Enforcing and
Administering Our Immigration Laws (two goals: strengthen and
effectively administer the immigration system; prevent unlaw-
ful immigration); 4) Safeguarding and Securing Cyberspace (two
goals: create a safe, secure, and resilient cyber environment; promote cybersecurity knowledge and innovation); and 5) Ensuring
Resilience to Disasters (4 goals: mitigate hazards, enhance preparedness, ensure effective emergency response, rapidly recover)
(p. i); references two key documents, the *National Infrastructure
Protection Plan* (NIPP) and the *National Response Framework* (NRF)
(p. A-1). In "Appendix A: Roles and Responsibilities across the
Homeland Security Enterprise," one finds a description of virtually every level of sovereignty, jurisdiction, and organization (i.e.,
federal, state, local, tribal, county, private sector, multinational
corporations, national voluntary organizations active in disaster
relief (NVOAD), NGOs, Communities, Individuals and Families,
including all emergency support functions (ESF) and ESF coordi-
nators based on the National Response Framework (p. A-9), and
all sector-specific agencies and the critical infrastructure and key

resource sectors they are charged with defending; for example, the Department of Energy (Energy), the DoD (Defense Industrial Base), Department of the Interior (National Monuments and Icons), as outlined in the National Infrastructure Protection Plan, which (p. A10). The QHSR Process (see Appendix B) is mandated by "Section 2401 of the Implementing Recommendations of the 9/11 Commission Act of 2007, [which] amends Title VII of the Homeland Security Act of 2002 to require the Secretary of Homeland Security to conduct a Quadrennial Homeland Security Review (QHSR) every 4 years beginning in 2009" (p. B-1). See also *Presidential Policy Directive/PPD-8, Subject: National Preparedness,* Washington, DC: The White House, March 30, 2011, available from *www.dhs.gov/presidential-policy-directive-8-national-preparedness;* and Jared T. Brown, Analyst in Emergency Management and Homeland Security Policy, *Presidential Policy Directive 8 and the National Preparedness System: Background and Issues for Congress,* Congressional Research Service (CRS), 7-5700, Washington, DC: 21 October 2011, available from *www.crs.gov.* See also *Department of Homeland Security Strategic Plan, Fiscal Years 2012-2016,* Washington, DC: U.S. Department of Homeland Security, February 2012, available from *www.dhs.gov/strategic-plan-fiscal-years-fy-2012-2016,* for description of five key missions: "secure our country from terrorist threats and enhance security; secure our borders; enforce our Nation's immigration laws; secure cyberspace; and build resilience to disasters" (p. i); a vision statement — "A homeland that is safe, secure, and resilient against terrorism and other hazards"; departmental mission:

> We will lead efforts to achieve a safe, secure, and resilient homeland. We will counter terrorism and enhance our security; secure and manage our borders; enforce and administer our immigration laws; protect cyber networks and critical infrastructure; and ensure resilience from disasters. We will accomplish these missions while providing essential support to national and economic security and maturing and strengthening both the Department of Homeland Security and the homeland security enterprise (p. 2);

and finally, its several mission goals and objectives.

50. The Honorable Matthew G. Olsen, Director, National Counterterrorism Center, *Hearing before the House Committee on*

Homeland Security, Understanding the Threat Landscape, Washington, DC: U.S. House of Representatives, July 25, 2012, esp. pp. 1-4.

51. Obama, "The Future of our Fight Against Terrorism."

52. National Security Preparedness Group, *Tenth Anniversary Report Card: The Status of the 9/11 Commission Recommendations,* Washington, DC: Bipartisan Policy Center, September 2011, available from *www.bipartisanpolicy.org/library/report/tenth-anniversary-report-card-status-911-commission-recommendations;* Cheryl Pellerin, "Officials: Defense-Intelligence Integration Strongest Since 9/11," Armed Forces Press Service, September 8, 2011, available from *www.defense.gov/news/newsarticle.aspx?id=65279.* Of these, several apply directly to this third strategic objective: the need for a unified incident command system to disaster response, radio spectrum and interoperability, deficiencies in the present passenger screening system, the need to standardize secure identification across states, develop better methods of identification, and develop uniform coalition standards for terrorist detention.

53. See "Homegrown Terrorism Cases, 2001-2013," Database compiled on plots, persons involved, and method of prevention, by the New America Foundation and Syracuse University's Maxwell School of Public Policy, including cases involving homegrown jihadist and non-jihadist terrorism in the United States since the 9/11 attacks; J. P. Bjelopera, *American Jihadist Terrorism: Combating a Complex Threat,* CRS Report for Congress, CRS 7-5700, Washington, DC: CRS, January 23, 2013.

54. Thirteen additional recommendations of the 2004 *9/11 Commission Report* deal with measures required to reorganize the federal government to achieve unity across a number of domains: unity of effort to bridge the foreign-domestic divide, unity of effort across the intelligence community, unity of effort in information sharing, and unity of effort in Congress. Of those, the vast majority are deemed sufficient. Establishment of the National Counterterrorism Center (NCTC) is key to remedying the foreign/domestic divide; unity across the intelligence communities provided by a CIA emphasis on human intelligence, language, culture, and diversity; and, DOD in charge of paramilitary operations, within the United States Special Operations Command (USSCOM); and, the overall budget allocation for intelligence be-

ing declassified; unity of information sharing promoted through the sharing of intelligence, and creation of a trusted information network for major national security institutions; unity of effort in Congress promoted by quicker national security appointments through new election cycles; and the organization of America's defenses to include that the FBI's national security focus and expertise is developed and enhanced, that DoD's oversight of U.S. Northern Command (NORTHCOM) is regularly assessed, and that Department of Homeland Security (DHS) oversight exists to assess and determine protection of critical infrastructure and the readiness of government response. Those few key areas in the realm of government organization still requiring improvement as of September 2011 include: need to create the Office of the Director of National Intelligence (ODNI), several recommendations directed at the U.S. Congress's process and organization (i.e., to fix the present dysfunctionality of those several major congressional committees charged with intelligence and counterterrorism [CT]), and need to create a single overall committee charged with oversight and review of homeland security.

55. For its original formulation as strategic objective, see *9/11 Commission Report*, pp. 374-383.

56. *Tenth Anniversary Report Card*, p. 7. Also, at p. 20: "Today, our country is undoubtedly safer and more secure than it was a decade ago. We have damaged the enemy, but the ideology of violent Islamist extremism is alive and attracting new adherents, including right here in our own country."

57. *National Strategy for Counterterrorism*, p. 1.

58. *Ibid.*, p. 3.

59. *Ibid.*, p. 4.

60. *Ibid.*, p. 10.

61. *Ibid.*, p. 11.

62. *Ibid.*, p. 15.

63. *Ibid.*, p. 17.

64. *Ibid.*, p. 19. For the importance of disaggregating the present AQ threat in those terms referred to above, see also Brian Michael Jenkins, "Getting the Threat Right," Santa Monica, CA: The RAND Corporation; Walter Pincus, "Sorting the terrorists," *The Washington Post*, December 12, 2012, available from *www.washingtonpost.com*.

65. Olsen cites as evidence the systematic degrading of Pakistan AQ leadership and operational capabilities; the May 2, 2011, death of Osama bin Laden; the August 2011 death of 'Atiyah 'Abd al-Rahman; the June 2012 killing of Abu Yahya al-Libi; other leaders driven underground and focused on security and survival and not terrorist plotting; and the fact that the London 2005 bombing was the last successful operation carried out by AQ in the West.

66. The Honorable Matthew G. Olsen, Director, National Counterterrorism Center, *Hearing before the House Committee on Homeland Security, Understanding the Threat Landscape*, Washington, DC: U.S. House of Representatives, July 25, 2012, p. 1.

67. *Ibid.*, pp. 2-6.

68. See Clapper, *Statement for the Record, Worldwide Threat Assessment of the US Intelligence Community*, pp. 3-6, 10.

69. Clapper further discusses AQ in Iraq, the al-Nusrah Front, Al-Shabaab, AQIM, Boko Haram, and the Lashkar i-Taybah in Pakistan as predominantly regional terrorist organizations that nevertheless have potentially regional ambitions that further threaten U.S. interests.

70. In reference to these affiliates, Obama states:

While we are vigilant for signs that these groups may pose a transnational threat, most are focused on operating in the countries and regions where they are based . That means we will face more localized threats like those we saw in Benghazi, or at the BP oil facility in Algeria, in which local operatives — in loose affiliation with regional networks — launch periodic attacks against Western diplomats, companies, and other soft targets, or resort to kidnapping and other criminal enterprises to fund their operations.

71. Obama, "The Future of our Fight Against Terrorism.

72. Analytical Support and Sanctions Monitoring Team, "Fourteenth Report of the Analytical Support and Sanctions Monitoring Team submitted pursuant to resolution 2083 (2012) concerning Al-Qaida and associated individuals and entities," New York: UN Security Council, S/2013/467, August 2, 2013, available from *www.un.org/ga/search/view_doc.asp?symbol=S/2013/467*. See also Associated Press, "UN Experts Say Al-Qaida Affiliates Remain a Threat," *The New York Times*, August 7, 2013, available from *www.nytimes.com*.

73. *Ibid.*, p. 5.

74. According to the New America Foundation and Maxwell School for Public Policy Report (see *homegrown.newamerica.net*), between September 11, 2001, and June 17, 2013, 212 of 390 persons indicted on terrorism-related charges or killed before an indictment could be handed down can be classified as "jihadist" terrorists, "and they subscribe broadly to the ideology of Osama bin Laden's al-Qaeda." The report lists 46 separate plots directed at the United States, and three directed outside the United States during that period.

75. *Ibid.*, p. 6.

76. *Ibid.*, p. 10.

77. Yoram Schweitzer and Aviad Mendelbaum, "Al-Qaeda: Vanquished or Strengthened?" *INSS Insight*, No. 456, August 13, 2013, available from *www.inss.org.il/index.aspx?id=4538&articleid=5428*.

78. Associated Press, "Man held in plot to blow up Federal Reserve," *Johnson City Press*, October 18, 2012, pp. 1A, 6A.

79. Wes Bruer, "Terror plot foiled in NYC," *Long War Journal*, November 21, 2011, available from *www.longwarjournal.org*.

80. Jamie Stengle, "Soldier shouts Hasan's name at hearing," *Johnson City Press*, July 30, 2011, p. 2A.

81. "Mass Shooting Threat Alleged," *Army Times*, June 21, 2010, p. 10.

82. Jess Bidgood, "Massachusetts Man Gets 17 Years in Terrorist Plot," *The New York Times*, November 2, 2012.

83. Michael Schwirz and Marc Santora, "Man is Accused of Jihadist Plot to Bomb a Bar in Chicago," *The New York Times*, September 15, 2012.

84. *Reuters*, "Second Man Gets 17 Years for Seattle Military Attack Plot," *The New York Times*, April 8, 2013.

85. *Reuters*, "Two Men Charged in Miami with Financing Foreign Terrorist Groups," *The New York Times*, August 15, 2013.

86. Associated Press, "UK Police Arrest 7 in Anti-Terror Operations," *The New York Times*, September 19, 2011, available from *www.nytimes.com*.

87. Scott Shane and Eric Schmitt, "Norway Announces Three Arrests in Terrorist Plot," *The New York Times*, July 8, 2010, available from *www.nytimes.com*.

88. John F. Burns, "3 Britons Convicted of Plot to Blow Up Airliners," *The New York Times*, July 8, 2010.

89. Selah Hennessy, "Stockholm Bomber 'Radicalized in Britain'," VOA News, December 3, 2010, available from *www.voanews. com/english/news/europe/Stockholm-Bomber-Radicalized-in-Britain-111797954.html*; Ravi Somaiya, "Swedish Bombing Suspect's Drift to Extremism," *The New York Times*, December 13, 2010.

90. Associated Press, "Canada Terror Suspect: Lawyer Must Use 'Holy Book'," *Stars and Stripes*, May 23, 2013.

91. Associated Press, "4 UK men jailed for discussing acts of terrorism," *Stars and Stripes*, April 18, 2013.

92. "Trial Begins for 3 British Islamists Accused of Bomb Plot," VOA News, October 22, 2012, available from *www.voanews.com*.

93. John F. Burns, "'Barbaric Attack' in London Prompts Meeting on Terror," *The New York Times*, May 22, 2013. See also Martin Robinson, "UK: Suspects in Woolwich Murder Case Part of 'Powerful Web of Islamic Radicals'," May 27, 2013, available from *www.opensource.gov*; Christopher Scheuermann, "Lessons from Woolwich: The Danger's of Britain's Islamist Underground," *Spiegel*, May 27, 2013, available from *www.spiegel.de/international/europe*. The suspects are quoted as saying:

> 'The only reason we have done this is because Muslims are dying every day' Adebolajo shouts into the camera, adding: 'The British soldier is an eye for an eye, a tooth for a tooth.'; To which the reported asks: 'How can it be that two young men who grew up in the UK could come to feel such hate?'

94. While this "foreign fighter" phenomenon has deep roots in the classical doctrine of defensive jihad, it also has shallower roots likely watered by an opportunistic AQ seeking to funnel fighters into the ranks of AQ's own violent cadre. It appears that the present Arab Spring tumult has led strategically to an AQ refocusing on the "near enemy," i.e., privileging the attacking of those forces thought to promote or tolerate infidelity or apostasy, that are geographically nearest, rather than the more distant "far enemy" ultimate enabler, the United States and the West generally. For important analyses of the foreign fighter phenomenon, globalized insurgency, and the return of the near enemy in AQ strategy, see Thomas Hegghammer, "The Rise of Muslim Foreign Fighters: Islam and the Globalization of Jihad," *International Security*, Vol. 35, No. 3, Winter 2010/2011, pp. 53-94; Thomas Hegghammer, "The Foreign Fighter Phenomenon: Islam and Transnational Militancy," Policy Brief, Cambridge, MA: Belfer Center for Science and International Affairs, Harvard Kennedy School, February 2011, available from *belfercenter.ksg.harvard.edu/publication/20713/foreign_fighter_phenomenon.html*; Michael P. Noonan, ed., *The Foreign Fighters: Problem, Recent Trends and Case Studies: Selected Essays*, Philadelphia, PA: FPRI, April 2011, available from *www.fpri.org*; Clint Watts, "Foreign Fighters: How Are They Being Recruited? Two Imperfect Recruitment Models," *Small Wars Journal*, June 22, 2008, available from *smallwarsjournal.com/blog/journal/docs-temp/69-watts.pdf?q=mag/docs-temp/69-watts.pdf*; Clint Watts, "Beyond Iraq and Afghanistan: What Foreign Fighter Data Reveals about the Future of Terrorism," *Small Wars Journal*,

April 17, 2008, available from *smallwarsjournal.com/blog/journal/ docs-temp/49-watts.pdf?q=mag/docs-temp/49-watts.pdf*; Clint Watts, "What If There is No Al-Qaeda? Preparing for Future Terrorism," Philadelphia, PA: FPRI, E-Notes, July 2012, available from *www. fpri.org/articles/2012/07/what-if-there-no-al-qaeda-preparing-future- terrorism.* For the phenomenon of "glocalization," see especially Christoph Reuter, "Terror Retooled: Al-Qaida Thinks Globally But Acts Locally," *Spiegel*, August 13, 2013, available from *www. spiegel.de/international/world.*

95. See, for examples, Anne Barnard and Eric Schmitt, "As Foreign Fighters Flood Syria, Fears of a New Extremist Haven," *The New York Times*, August 8, 2013, available from *www.nytimes. com*; Thomas Hegghammer, "Syria's Foreign Fighters," *Foreign Policy*, December 9, 2013, available from *mideastafrica.foreignpolicy. com/posts/2013/12/09/syrias_foreign_fighers*; BBC News, "Hundreds of Britons fighting in Syria—MI5 Chief," November 7, 2013; Greg Miller, "U.S. charges 14 with giving support to Somali insurgent group," *The Washington Post*, August 6, 2010, available from *www. washingtonpost.com*; Bill Roggio, "American who fought for Al Nusrah Front arrested in US," *Long War Journal*, March 29, 2013, available from *www.longwarjournal.org* (the individual involved, Harroun, was known in Syria as "the American" and was a for- mer American soldier); Bill Roggio, "American passport found at al Qaeda base in northern Syria," *Long War Journal*, July 23, 2013, available from *www.longwarjournal.org* (the passport belonged to 'Amir Farouk Ibrahim, born in Pennsylvania on October 30, 1989; the passport was issued March 6, 2012); Bill Roggio, "Ameri- can Shabab fighter urges Muslims to join the 'fronts' of jihad," *Long War Journal*, February 27, 2013, available from *www.longwar journal.com*, (the "American, who is identified as Abu Ahmed al Amriki, is seen on a videotape that was produced by Shabaab's media arm and posted on jihadist Internet forums. . . . Abu Ahmed implores Muslims to leave their lives of comfort and wage jihad in Somalia, Mali, Afghanistan, Iraq, or the 'Islamic Maghreb'—North Africa"). See also Clint Watts, "Radicalization in the U.S. Beyond al Qaeda: Treating the disease of disconnection," Philadelphia, PA: FPRI, August 2012, available from *www.fpri.org*; Waqar Gil- lani and Sabrina Tavernise, "5 Americans Sentenced to 10 Years in Pakistani Prison," *The New York Times*, June 25, 2010, p. A4: "The five men, all in their 20s and all from Virginia, are believed by Pakistani and American law enforcement officials to have trav-

eled to Pakistan in December to join the fight against American forces in Afghanistan"; Scott Shane and Eric Schmitt, "One Drone Victim's Trail from Raleigh to Pakistan," *The New York Times*, May 22, 2013; Jude Kenan Mohammad, at 18 under influence of Daniel Patrick Boyd—"charged in 2009 as ringleader of a group of North Carolina residents who had vowed to carry out violent jihad both in the United States and overseas"—was killed in a drone strike in South Waziristan at age 23 on November 16, 2011. He was the fourth American to die in a drone strike, the other three were Anwar al-Awlaki, specifically targeted, but Samir Khan, "another young man from Raleigh who had joined the Qaeda branch in Yemen . . . [and] Awlaki's 16-year-old son, Abdulrahman, killed 2 weeks later; and Mr. Mohammad." Mohammed was killed in a "signature strike," i.e., a strike carried out on the basis of a signature, an activity indicative of terrorist-related activity but not provide the identification of the specific perpetrators involved.

96. For a comprehensive recent review of this vast literature, see Dr. Alex P. Schmid, "Radicalisation, De-Radicalisation, Counter-Radicalisation: A Conceptual Discussion and Literature Review," *ICCT Research Paper*, International Centre for Counter-Terrorism—The Hague, The Czech Republic, March 2013, available from *www.icct.nl*.

97. Marc Sageman, *Leaderless Jihad: Terrorist Networks in the Twenty-First Century*, Philadelphia, PA: University of Pennsylvania Press, 2009, Chap. 1.

98. *Ibid.*, pp. viii, 154-156.

99. See Scott Atran, "Genesis of Suicide Terrorism," *Science*, 2003, p. 1537; Ann Speckhard, Beatrice Jacuch, and Valentijn Vanrompay, "Taking on the Persona of a Suicide Bomber: a Thought Experiment," *Perspectives on Terrorism*, May 2012, Vol. 6, No. 2, p. 58; Robert A. Pape and James A. Feldman, *Cutting the Fuse: The Explosion of Global Suicide Terrorism and How to Stop It*, Chicago, IL: University of Chicago Press, pp. 58-60; Hegghammer, "Syria's Foreign Fighters."

100. See Albert Bandura, "Mechanisms of Moral Disengagement," Walter Reich, ed., *Origins of Terrorism: Psychologies, Ideologies, Theologies, States of Mind*, Washington, DC: Woodrow Wilson Center Press; Distributed by Johns Hopkins University Press,

Baltimore, MD, and London, UK: pp. 161-191, for how having on the basis of fabrication, disinformation, and terrorist propaganda reconstrued one's actions as morally based, and one's moral indignation fully justified, normal human beings are able to kill. For additional adumbrations of this argument, see Albert Bandura, Claudio Barbaranelli, Gian Vittorio Caprara, and Concetta Pastorelli, "Mechanisms of Moral Disengagement in the Exercise of Moral Agency," *Journal of Personality and Social Psychology*, 1996; Albert Bandura, "Selective Moral Disengagement in the Exercise of Moral Agency," *Journal of Moral Education*, 2002, Vol. 31, No. 2, pp. 101-119; Michael J. Osofsky, Albert Bandura, and Philip G. Zimbardo, "The Role of Moral Disengagement in the Execution Process," *Law and Human Behavior*, 2005, Vol 29, No. 4, pp. 371-393. See also Ann Speckhard *et al.*, "Taking on the Persona of a Suicide Bomber: a Thought Experiment," *Perspectives in Terrorism*, May 2012, Vol. 6, No. 2, pp. 51-73, for a very interesting, though low-power, study examining the relationship between propaganda, moral outrage, and the willingness to kill.

101. For the importance of affective variables, particularly anger/moral outrage, as relevant to the process of radicalization, see Stephen K. Rice, "Emotions and terrorism research: A case for a social-psychological agenda," *Journal of Criminal Justice*, 2009, Vol. 37, pp. 248-255; David Wright-Neville and Debra Smith, "Political rage: terrorism and the politics of emotion," *Global Change, Peace & Security*, 2009, Vol. 21, No. 1, pp. 85-98. For the notion that revenge-seeking based on moral indignation is most likely a human universal, see Brian Knutson, "Sweet Revenge?" *Science*, August 27, 2004, Vol. 305, pp. 1246-1247.

102. This well-known Southern U.S. colloquialism shall serve us well. A pig, regardless of how beautifully painted with the most embellished of tones (read: rhetoric, spin, misrepresentation), remains after all, a pig. I apologize beforehand to my Muslim and Jewish compatriots for whom this animal signifies extreme ritual impurity, and request only deference to a highly useful notion that so quickly cuts through hypocritical muck.

103. *Primer/Fundamentals of Information Operations*, November 2009, AY10 Ed., Carlisle, PA: U.S. Army War College, p. 9. A fuller re-bureaucratized definition is also provided in *Ibid.*, p. 9:

[F]ocused United States Government processes and efforts to understand and engage key audiences in order to create, strengthen, or preserve conditions favorable to advance national interests and objectives through the use of coordinated information, themes, plans, programs, and actions synchronized with other elements of national power.

104. *Ibid.*, p. 13; See also Michael Egner, "Social Science Foundations for Strategic Communications in the Global War on Terrorism," Paul K. Davis and Kim Cragin, eds., *Social Science for Counterterrorism: putting the pieces together,* Santa Monica, CA: The RAND Corporation, p. 354.

Ultimately, actions speak louder than words, and good communication can only partially mitigate the effects of an unpopular policy or action. Indeed, it is paradoxically when words are needed the most—during a crisis or when the credibility of a messenger is on the line—that the effectiveness of mere 'spin' drops even further.

See also pp. 344-348.

105. "Pentagon propaganda plan is source of controversy," available from *usatoday30.usatoday.com/NEWS/usaedition.*

106. *Information Operations Primer*, p. 1. IO includes 13 distinct capabilities: five core (PSYOP, Military Deception, Operations Security, Electronic Warfare, Computer Network Operations), five supporting (Information Assurance, Physical Security, Physical attack, Counterintelligence, and Combat Camera), and three related (Public Affairs, Civil-Military Operations, and Defense Support to Public Diplomacy). *Ibid.*, pp. 4-6.

107. *Ibid.*, p. 7. For other definitions of strategic communications, see *www.au.af.mil/info-ops/strategic.htm;* "United States Strategic Communication," available from *en.wikipedia.org/wiki/United_States_Strategic_Communication;* "Strategic Communication," DoD definition, *Joint Publication 5-0,* available from *www.dtic.mil/doctrine/dod_dictionary/data/s/18179.html;* U.S. Joint Forces Command, Joint Warfighting Center, *Commander's Handbook for Strategic Communication and Communication Strategy,* Version, Carlisle, PA: U.S. Army War College, June 24, 2010.

108. Richard Holbrooke, "Get the Message Out," *The Washington Post*, op-ed, October 28 2011, available from *www. washingtonpost.com*.

109. *Ibid*.

110. A similar unwillingness to question publically U.S. policies vis–à–vis the Israel-Palestine confrontation and its possible role in undercutting U.S. credibility and elevating that of bin Laden was displayed in the *9/11 Commission Report*, p. 174. According to the follow-up volume by Committee co-chairs Thomas A. Kean and Lee H. Hamilton in describing the Commission's inside-story, this was the result of a "compromise." See Thomas A. Kean and Lee H. Hamilton, *Without Precedent: The Inside Story of the 9/11 Commission*, New York: Alfred A. Knopf, 2006, pp. 284-285. They state:

> We did, however, have some disagreement over foreign policy issues. Much of it revolved around the question of Al Qaeda's motivation. For instance, Lee felt that there had to be an acknowledgment that a settlement of the Israeli-Palestinian conflict was vital to America's long-term relationship with the Islamic world, and that the presence of American forces in the Middle East was a major motivating factor in al Qaeda's actions. . . . This was sensitive ground. Commissioners who argued that al Qaeda was motivated primarily by religious ideology – and not by opposition to American policies – rejected mentioning the Israeli-Palestinian conflict in the report. In their view, listing U.S. support for Israel as a root cause of Al Qaeda's opposition to the United States indicated that the United States should reassess that policy. To Lee, though, it was not a question of altering support for Israel but of merely stating a fact that the Israeli-Palestinian conflict was central to the relations between the Islamic world and the United States – and to Bin Ladin's ideology and the support he gained throughout the Islamic world for his jihad against America.

Moreover, the *9/11 Commission Report* does acknowledge, at least with respect to Khalid Sheik Muhammad (KSM), this motivation:

> [Ramzi] Yousef's instant notoriety as the mastermind of the 1993 World Trade Center bombing inspired KSM to become

127

involved in planning attacks against the United States. By his own account, KSM's animus toward the United States stemmed not from his experiences there as a student, but rather from his violent disagreement with U.S. foreign policy favoring Israel.

The willingness **not** to put lipstick on pigs vis-à-vis U.S. foreign policies in the Arab and Muslim world is evident in a remarkable memo by Jude Wanniski ("The Mind of a Terrorist," available from *www.wnd.com/2001/09/10813*). This eerily prescient 1998 letter was originally sent to then-Senator Jesse Helms (R-NC), on the occasion of the sentencing of 1993 World Trade Center bombing mastermind Ramzi Yousef. It was later forwarded as a memo on September 12, 2001, at 1 a.m. to then Vice President Dick Cheyney.

111. *Ibid.*

112. Kamolnick, *Delegitimizing Al-Qaeda*; Paul Kamolnick, "Al Qaeda's Sharia Crisis: Sayyid Imam and the Jurisprudence of Lawful Military Jihad," *Studies in Conflict and Terrorism*, 2013, Vol. 36, pp. 394-318; Paul Kamolnick, "The Egyptian Islamic Group's Critique of Al Qaeda's Interpretation of Jihad," *Perspectives on Terrorism*, Vol. 7, No. 5, 2013, pp. 93-110.

113. Holbrooke, "Get the Message Out."

114. In contrast to Holbrooke's puzzlement, consider Abdelwahab al-Affendi's incisive observation: "When the country which commands unchallenged hegemony in both the technology and the art of communication appears unable to get its message across, it can only be a symptom of a deeper concern." See Abdelwahab el-Affendi, "The Conquest of Muslim Hearts and Minds? *Perspectives on U.S. Reform and Public Diplomacy Strategies*, September 1, 2005, p. iv, available from *www.brookings.edu/research/papers/2005/09/islamicworld-el-affendi*.

115. Office of the Under Secretary of Defense for Acquisition, Technology and Logistics, Report of the Defense Science Board Task Force, Washington, DC: DoD, September 2004, *Strategic Communication*, available from *www.acq.osd.mil/dsb/reports/ADA428770.pdf*. An earlier study (see Office of the Under Secretary of Defense for Acquisition, Technology and Logistics, Report

of the Defense Science Board Task Force, *Managed Information Dissemination*, Washington, DC: DoD, October 2001, available from *www.au.af.mil/au/awc/awcgate/dod/dsb_managed_info_dissem.pdf*) did not discuss terrorism or AQ, or radical Islam's ascendency and potential challenge to U.S. vital interests. Its primary objective was to examine short-comings in U.S. information operations during contingency operations in Darfur, Haiti, Iraq, but especially the Balkan conflicts.

116. Defense Science Board Task Force, September 2004, *Strategic Communication*, esp. pp. 14-18, 33-47, 84.

117. For a comprehensive examination of this public opinion, see Steven Kull, *Feeling Betrayed: The Roots of Muslim Anger at America*, Washington, DC: The Brookings Institution, 2011.

118. *Ibid.*

119. Defense Science Board Task Force, September 2004, *Strategic Communication*, p. 40.

120. *Ibid.*, p. 35.

121. *Ibid.*

122. *Ibid.*, p. 43.

123. *Ibid.*, p. 61.

124. *Ibid.*, p. 51.

125. Under Secretary for Public Diplomacy and Public Affairs, Strategic Communication and Public Diplomacy Policy Coordinating Committee (PCC), *U.S. National Strategy for Public Diplomacy and Strategic Communication*, Washington, DC: U.S. Department of State, June 2007, available from *www.au.af.mil/au/awc/awcgate/state/natstrat_strat_comm.pdf*.

126. *Ibid.*, esp, pp. 7, 12-13.

127. *Ibid.*, pp. 8, 10, 17, 31, 32.

128. See, for example, Jon Armajani, *Modern Islamist Movements: History, Religion, and Politics*, Oxford, UK: Wiley-Blackwell, 2012; Mohammed Ayoob, *The Many Faces of Political Islam: Religion and Politics in the Muslim World*, Ann Arbor, MI: The University of Michigan Press, 2008; Noah Feldman, *After Jihad: America and the Struggle for Islamic Democracy*, New York, Farrar, Straus, and Giroux, 2003; Noah Feldman, *The Fall and Rise of the Islamic State*, Princeton, NJ, and Oxford, UK: Princeton University Press, 2008; Ahmad S. Moussalli, *The Islamic Quest for Democracy, Pluralism, and Human Rights*, Gainesville, FL: University Presses of Florida, 2001; Abdullah Ahmed An-Na'im, *Islam and the Secular State: Negotiating the Future of Shari'a*, Cambridge, MA: Harvard University Press, 2008.

129. Office of the Secretary of Under Secretary for Defense for Acquisition, Technology, and Logistics, *Report of the Defense Science Board Task Force on Strategic Communication*, Washington, DC: DoD, January 2008, available from *www.au.af.mil/au/awc/awcgate/dod/dsb_strategic_comm_jan08.pdf*. See also in the same document, "Appendix E. Government and Independent Organization Studies of Strategic Communication and Public Diplomacy, September 2001-October 2007," for a listing of 36 reports, 14 by the Government Accountability Office (GAO), authored over this period.

130. *Ibid.*, esp. Chap. 3, pp. 29-37.

131. *Ibid.*, p. 39.

132. *Ibid.*, p. 81.

133. See Office of the President of the United States, *National Framework for Strategic Communication*, 2010, Washington, DC: The White House, available from *www.fas.org/man/eprint/pubdip.pdf*; *GAO-12-612R Strategic Communication*, Washington, DC: U.S. Government Accountability Office (GAO), May 2012, available from *www.gao.gov/assets/600/591123.pdf*; Office of the President of the United States, *Update to Congress on National Framework for Strategic Communication*, Washington, DC: The White House, 2012, available from *www.hsdl.org/?view&did=704809*.

134. Office of the President of the United States, *National Framework for Strategic Communication*, p. 1.

135. *Ibid.*

136. Office of the President of the United States, *National Framework for Strategic Communication*, p. 2. It is interesting to note how diminished this conception is in relation to the far more robust conception of strategic communication, and of its potential modalities and instruments of national power, in the *Information Operations Primer*. On p. 9, strategic communication is defined as:

> focused United States Government processes and efforts to understand and engage key audiences in order to create, strengthen, or preserve conditions favorable to advance national interests and objectives through the use of coordinated information, themes, plans, programs, and actions synchronized with other elements of national power. . . . Parsing this rather bureaucratic definition to its essentials, strategic communication is the orchestration of actions, words, and images to achieve cognitive effects in support of policy and military objectives;

> Strategic communication is simply a way to affect perceptions, attitudes and behaviors of key audiences in support of objectives. Certainly communications means are very important in ultimately achieving those desired information effects. But how military operations are conducted or policy is implemented is also a key component of strategic communication, since actions send very loud and clear messages (p. 13).

137. *Ibid.*, pp. 2-3.

138. *Ibid.*, p. 2.

139. *Ibid.*, p. 3.

140. *Ibid.*, pp. 3-4.

141. The remainder of this document deals with the organizational implications of this proposal and discusses the many USG agencies charged with various dimensions of influence operations and information operations, including: the Senior Director for Global Engagement (SDGE) in Deputy National Security Advisor for Strategic Communications (DNSA/SC), Department of State, Department of Defense, Broadcasting Board of Governors

responsible for "non-military, international broadcasting sponsored by the United States Government" (p. 11); U.S. Agency for International Development (USAID), Intelligence Community, NCTC (The Global Engagement Group, Directorate of Strategic Operational Planning at NCTC).

142. Office of the Secretary of Under Secretary for Defense for Acquisition, Technology, and Logistics, *Report of the Defense Science Board Task Force on Strategic Communication.*

143. Phyllis D'Hoop, ed., *An Initiative: Strengthening U.S.-Muslim Communications*, Washington, DC: Center for the Study of the American Presidency, July 2003.

144. *Ibid.*, pp. 4-5.

145. *Ibid.*, p. 5.

146. *Ibid.*, p. 12. See also especially, "Principal Sources of Anti-Americanism in the Muslim World," pp. 102-122, a powerful but representative comment of which is the following in reference to the need to encourage representative governance in Muslim countries (p. 114):

> If U.S. policies toward the Palestinian issue are the most important reason for resentment of the United States, the second reason is the anger and the frustration over our support for autocratic regimes in the region. I [Dr. Masmoudi, President, The Center for the Study of Islam and Democracy] think this is a big reason. I also think that it is very closely related to the Palestinian-Israeli issue, the reason being we are seen as hypocrites. While we have talk about human rights, democracy and freedom, in the Arab world, we have, in fact, been supporting autocratic regimes that are not representative, not elected and not accountable to anybody.

147. Report of the Advisory Group on Public Diplomacy for the Arab and Muslim World, *Changing Minds, Winning Peace: A New Strategic Direction for U.S. Public Diplomacy in the Arab & Muslim World*, Washington, DC: U.S. Department of State, October 1, 2003, p. 9, available from *www.state.gov/documents/organization/2488s.pdf.* The unenviable Machiavellianism required to "sell" such policies seems the task of this particular advisory

group. For example, on one hand, they state, "We must also confront the contradiction that troubles believers in democracy and liberalization. They see official U.S. diplomacy as frequently buttressing governments hostile to freedom and prosperity." So what is the role of public diplomacy in such a situation, one might ask? The answer (p. 18) is:

> Public diplomacy gives the United States the opportunity to supplement the support of such regimes — often a policy necessity — with broader, long-term promotion of universal values and economic, political, and social reforms that directly support public aspirations.

See pp. 19-24 also, for what to this author are similarly contradictory and unconvincing attempts to espouse and defend values that are directly undermined by present policy commitments. Another similarly unconvincing set of reports admits on one hand the importance of policy, yet seeks on the other to "put lipstick on pigs" through effective communications. It states:

> Although this paper does not tackle the U.S. foreign and domestic policy issues that drive global and Islamic world public perceptions of America, it does acknowledge that our policies are central determinants of global views. Nonetheless, how we communicate, including methods and our posture of humility — or lack thereof — remains a central part of how we tackle the problems of public diplomacy and it is these methods that this paper will examine.

See Hady Amr, *The Need to Communicate: How to Improve U.S. Public Diplomacy with the Islamic World*, Analysis Paper #6, Washington, DC: The Saban Center for Middle East Policy, The Brookings Institution, January 2004, p. 8. See also Hady Amr and P. W. Singer, *Restoring America's Good Name: Improving Strategic Communications with the Islamic World*, Washington, DC: The Brookings Institution, August 2006, available from *www.brookings.edu/research/papers/2006/09/middleeast-amr*; Hady Amr and P. W. Singer, *Engaging the Muslim World: A Communication Strategy to Win the War of Ideas*, Washington, DC: The Brookings Institution, April 2007. For an outstanding, insightful, starkly contrasting approach supporting a transformation in U.S. policies toward support for the democratic and reformist Islamist forces rather than efforts to mask present contradictions pitting pro-authoritarian or authoritarian-tolerant policy and democratic rhetoric, see Abdelwahab el-Affendi, *The Conquest of Muslim Hearts and Minds? Perspectives on U.S. Reform and Public Diplomacy Strategies*, Washington, DC: The Brookings Institution, September 1, 2005, available from *www.brookings.edu/research/papers/2005/09/islamicworld-el-affendi*. For example, el-Affendi, remarks (p. 2): "The link between Islamism and terrorism is at best contingent. The problem, in fact, relates more to widespread anti-Americanism based on some U.S. policies or popular perceptions of them." In reference to the present crisis of U.S. credibility and public diplomacy (p. 2):

> The starting point of this process [reforming US public diplomacy] is the recognition of the dysfunctional role, lack of legitimacy, and unrepresentativeness that characterizes the state as a structure in much of the Muslim world. This condition is demonstrated by the primacy of the U.S. public diplomacy campaign, which is directed toward the general Muslim public, rather than the governments in the Muslim world. This indicates the existence of a moral and institutional vacuum at the heart of the region's political landscape.

See also "A Credibility Problem," pp. 7-10.

148. The Arab-Israel confrontation, and more specific Palestinian struggle for national rights and against occupation, is one of the most significant historical sources of modern terrorism. See Bureau of Public Affairs, Office of the Historian, "Historical Background: Significant Terrorist Incidents, 1961-2003: A Brief Chronology," Washington, DC: Department of State, 2013, available from *www.fas.org/irp/threat/terror_chron.html*; Judith Colp Rubin and Caroline Taillandier, "Appendix: Chronology of Middle East-Connected Terrorism Against Americans [c. 1961-2001]," Barry Rubin and Judith Colp Rubin, eds., *Anti-American Terrorism and the Middle East: A Documentary History*, New York: Oxford University Press, 2002, pp. 351-366.

149. Further confidence in this conclusion arises from the fact that it is by no means a radical opinion maintained by an unhinged fringe of the political left or right. Rather, this conclusion is arrived at by persons with varying sorts of commitments and institutional affiliation, e.g., Arab and Muslim academics, non-Arab and non-Muslim academics and analysts, U.S. military and intelligence analysts, and persons of varying political ideologi-

cal orientations. For a very brief but indicative sampling beyond those already summarized, see Mustapha Kamel Al-Sayyid, *The Other Face of the Islamist Movement*, Working Papers, Democracy and Rule of Law Project, Global Policy Forum, Washington, DC: Carnegie Endowment for International Peace, No. 23, January 2003, esp. pp. 26-27, available from *www.carnegieendowment. org/files/wp33.pdf*; Said Amir Arjomand, "Can Rational Analysis Break a Taboo: A Middle Eastern Perspective," Eric Hershberg and Kevin W. Moore, *Critical Views of September 11: Analyses from Around the World*, New York, Social Science Research Council, The New Press, pp. 162-176; Robert Art and Louise Richardson, eds., *Democracy and Counterterrorism: lessons from the past*, "Conclusion," Washington, DC: United States Institute of Peace Press, esp. pp. 592-596; Bari Atwan, *The Secret History of al Qaeda*, Updated edition, Berkeley and Los Angeles, CA: University of California Press, 2008 (orig. 2006), esp. pp. 294-298; Martha Crenshaw, "Why America? The Globalization of Civil War," *Current History*, December 2001, pp. 425-432; Robert Fisk, "Our Actions in the Middle East are What is Endangering Our Security," *The Independent*, November 6, 2010, available from *www.commondreams.org/ view/2010/11/06-2?print*; Graham E. Fuller, "The Future of Political Islam," *Foreign Affairs*, March/April 2002, available from *www. foreignaffairs.com/print/57806*; Fawaz A. Gerges, *America and Political Islam: Clash of Cultures or Clash of Interests*, Cambridge, UK, and New York: Cambridge University Press, 1999; Simon Haddad and Hilal Khashan, "Islam and Terrorism: Lebanese Muslim Views on September 11," *Journal of Conflict Resolution*, Vol. 46, No. 6, December 2002, pp. 812-828; Muhammad Haniff Bin Hassan, "Key Considerations in Counterideological Work against Terrorist Ideology," *Studies in Conflict and Terrorism*, Vol. 29, 2006, esp. pp. 548-549; Thomas H. Kean and Lee H. Hamilton, *Without Precedent: The Inside Story of the 9/11 Commission*, New York, Alfred A. Knopf, 2006, esp. pp. 284-285; Michael B. Meyer, Major, USAF, *America's Credibility at Stake: Arab Perceptions of US Foreign Policy*, A Research Report Submitted to Faculty in Partial Fulfillment of the Graduation Requirements, Maxwell Air Force Base, AL: Air and Staff Command College, Air University, March 19, 2002; Mahmood Mamdani, "Good Muslim, Bad Muslim: A Political Perspective on Culture and Terrorism," Eric Hershberg and Kevin W. Moore, *Critical Views of September 11*, pp. 44-60; Major Roy P. Matur, USAF, *Influencing Transnational Terrorist Organizations: Using Influence Nets to Prioritize Factors*, June 2005, Graduate

Research Project in Partial Fulfillment for the Degree of Masters of Operational Sciences, AFIT/GOS/ENS/05-06, Wright-Patterson Air Force Base, OH: Air University, Department of the Air Force, Air Force Institute of Technology, esp. pp. iv, 16-31, available from *www.au.af.mil/au/awc/awcgate/afit/fatur_influences_terrorists.pdf*; Clark McCauley and Sophia Moskalenko, "Recent U.S. Thinking About Terrorism," *Terrorism and Political Violence*, 2010, Vol. 22, esp. 647; Robert Pape, *Dying to Win: The Logic of Suicide Terrorism*, Chicago, IL: University of Chicago Press, 2005; Robert Pape and J. Feldman, *Cutting the Fuse: The Explosion of Suicide Terrorism and How to Stop It*, Chicago, IL: University of Chicago Press, 2010; PEW Global Attitudes Project, December 19 2001; Marc Sageman, *Leaderless Jihad: Terrorist networks in the 21st Century*, Philadelphia, PA: University of Pennsylvania Press, 2009, esp. p. 35-36; Brent J. Talbot and Michael B. Meyer, *View from the East: Arab Perceptions of United States Presence and Policy*, Institute for National Security Studies (INSS) Occassional Paper No. 48, USAF Academy, CO: USAF Institute for National Security Studies, February 2003; Sherifa Zuhur, *Precision in the Global War on Terror: Inciting Muslims Through the War of Ideas*, Carlisle, PA: Strategic Studies Institute, U.S. Army War College, April 2008, available from *www.StrategicStudiesInstitute.army.mil*, esp. p. 118.

150. See also Kamolnick, *Delegitimizing Al-Qaeda*, note 72, pp. 59-64 (Simon Reeve, *The New Jackals: Ramzi Yousef, Osama bin Laden, and the future of terrorism*, Boston, MA: Northeastern University Press, 1999, "Appendix Three: A letter from Ramzi Yousef and the other conspirators in the World Trade Center bombing, published as received by *The New York Times* 4 days after the February 1993 explosion," pp. 274-275): "Ramzi Yousef, mastermind of the 1993 World Trade Center plot, as well as others, including the initial planning of the 'Planes Operation' — who had earlier failed in an attempt to bomb the Israeli embassy in Bangkok, Thailand, and whose initial New York targets were not the World Trade Center but targeting Jewish neighborhoods in Crown Heights and Williamsburg— had this to say as a final statement following his conviction for that crime:

We are, the fifth battalion in the Liberation Army, declare our responsibility for the explosion on the mentioned building. This action was done in response for the American political, economical and military support to Israel the state of terrorism and to the rest of the dictator countries in the region.

Our demands:
Stop all military, economical, and political aids [sic] to Israel.
All diplomatic relations with Israel must stop.
Not to interfere with any of the Middle East countries [sic] interior affairs.
. . . The terrorism that Israel practices (which is supported by America) must be faced with a similar one. The dictatorship and terrorism (also supported by America) that some countries are practicing against their own people must also be faced with terrorism.

The American people must know, that their civilians who got killed are not better than those who are getting killed by the American weapons and support.

The American people are responsible for the actions of their government and they must question all of the crimes that their government is committing against other people. Or they – Americans – will be the targets of our operations that could diminish them.

We invite all of the people from all countries and all of the revolutionaries in the world to participate in this action with us to accomplish our just goals.

'IF THEN ANYONE TRANSGRESSES THE PROHIBITION AGAINST YOU TRANSGRESS YE LIKEWISE AGAINST HIM. . . .

Al-Farbek Al-Rokn,
Abu Bakr Al-Makee

CNN, in its write-up of the final verdict, represented facts by stating: "After 3 days of deliberation in November, a federal jury convicted Yousef and Eyad Ismoil on murder and conspiracy charges for their roles in a plot by Islamic extremists to topple the trade centers two 110-story [sic] towers to punish the United States for its support of Israel," available from *articles.cnn.com/1998-01-08/us/980108 yousef 1 trade-center-bombing-yousef-and-eyad-ismoil-conviction-S=PM:US*. Finally, at least one of the East Africa Embassy bombers made his motives known in published transcripts of the case (See *United States of America v. Usama bin Laden, et al.,* S(7) 98 Cr. 1023, United States District Court, Southern District of New York, New York, N.Y., October 18, 2001, Sentencing hearing, available from *fl1.findlaw.com/news/findlaw.com/cnn/docs/binladen/*

usbinldn101801.) El Hage's complicity in the attacks was proved, but based on his testimony one learns that policy, not shari'a, primarily motivated him; also, that the killing of innocent human beings — something he apparently did not know would happen — is absolutely unacceptable under Islamic law. The defendants, Wadih El Hage, Mohamed Sadeek Odeh, Mohamed Rashed Daoud Al-'Owhali, and Khalfan Khamis Mohamed, all received life without parole: Odeh's views (see p. 112) are referred to by Judge Leonard B. Sand when he states as their motives, "Mr. Odeh's opposition to United States' support of Israel, financially, politically and militarily, [and] presence of the United States military in the holy lands of Saudi Arabia, [and] the Persian Gulf and the Horn of Africa . . ." At p. 113, Judge Sands states: "The attack may have been intended to attack American foreign policy, but the victims were innocent people. . . ." At pp. 115-116, the distinction is made between support of al-Qaeda's military goals and deep regret at loss of innocent civilian life. Odeh's attorney, Anthony L. Ricco, states:

> He is now prepared to face the sentence that the court must impose here. He is very much aware of the substantial human loss that occurred here. He is not oblivious to the fact that many people were injured and many people died here who were innocent. He acknowledged that very early on in the case when he was interrogated. He has always expressed that. He does not have remorse, your Honor, about his participation in Al Qaeda. That's a difference in his mind. . . . Mohamed Odeh has always stated that he was not a part of the execution of the bombing. He continues in that position today, but that does not mean, your Honor, that he is a person who is oblivious to the great loss of human life and the great injury that was inflicted upon people here (pp. 115-116).

El-Hage, a second defendant, addressed the Court before his sentencing with a very revealing, fundamentalist narrative, but one that appears to recognize the enormity of killing innocents and indeed one that exhibits moral revulsion. His view of the United States is positive from a Muslim perspective: he repeatedly refers to the United States as a land where Islam can be freely spread and practiced ("Others chose to migrate to other countries, such as the U.S., where they can spread the message of Islam freely and in the same time support their brothers and sisters who are continuing their efforts to apply God's rules in the Islamic countries," p. 139); also: "Islam became the fastest growing religion in the U.S., as it is in the whole world, all praise be to God first, and to the tolerant, open society here" (p. 139); also:

Now, even though the Islamic system and way of life is for the best of all humanity [sic], devout Muslims, as I believe, are not asking to apply it here in the U.S., where Muslims are less than 7 million. They are a minority. The fact is that they want to apply it in the Islamic countries where the majority are Muslims. But in those countries, today's selfish, arrogant and self-deceited kings, presidents and rulers want to apply their own self-invented rules . . . [T]o make the long story short [sic], by the 20th century, the rulers started to neglect the Koranic laws, substituting them with manmade [sic] laws. The result is what we see today. Muslim nations are the weakest, poorest and most miserable. That is why, in my opinion, we find devout, committed Muslims, individuals and groups, working actively to reimplement God's rules and guidance (pp. 137-138).

As for moral revulsion: "[D]evout Muslims, . . even in time of conflict, they should not exceed certain limits, harming innocent people or noncombatant ones. This is very stressed upon [sic] in the Koran and the teachings of the prophet Muhammad, peace be upon him, who even prohibited destroying crops, animals or property at time of war" (p. 139); and again:

When the bombings happened in Africa in '98, my opinion was that that action was extreme and not in accordance with the beliefs that I learned. I made my opinion clear well before I was arrested or charged. Today, my opinion is still the same towards what happened in Africa and what happened here last month (September 11, 2001 [9/11]. The killing of innocent people and noncombatant is radical, extreme and cannot be tolerated by any religion, principles, beliefs or values. Today I can stand here and say that I did not participate or support any extreme conduct or any act that violates my beliefs as a devout Muslim...(pp. 141-142).

El-Hage, at pp. 142-143, identifies "many American policies towards Muslim countries [that] are wrong" including the alleged "over one million child [sic] and thousands of innocent people" affected by the embargo on Iraq; "the unconditional support of the American government to the Israeli government that is killing innocent Palestinians, taking their land, expelling them and destroying their homes" (p. 142); the effect on deeply religious Muslims of "having non-Muslim troops on the land of Muslims' holiest sites, its negative impact on Muslim masses around the world and specifically those on the Arabian Peninsula" (p. 142). He goes on to also say though:

> Such policies, in my opinion, are wrong and end up breeding unjustified extremism. . . . Many Muslims and non-Muslims have expressed the same views. That includes the American Muslim community, which I am a member of, which is free to voice its criticism to the American policy [sic] but without committing or supporting any extreme acts (pp. 142-143).

In his defense, he also states: "I am still the person who avoids radical solutions and acts, as I did in the past" (p. 145). (El-Hage had at that time no prior record of any violent or illegal activity.)

151. Holbrooke, "Get the Message Out."

152. Obama, "The Future of our Fight Against Terrorism."

153. *Joint Publication (JP) 1-02, Department of Defense Dictionary of Military and Associated Terms*, November 8, 2010, As Amended Through 15 April 2012, Washington, DC: DoD; from JP 3-13-2.

154. A very insightful analysis of a triangular structure that links violence or the threat of violence, mass communication, and feelings of chronic fear (terror), can be found in Alex P. Schmid, "The Response Problem as a Definition Problem," *Terrorism and Political Violence*, Vol. 4, No. 4, pp. 7-13, especially p. 10, Figure 1, "The Triangle of Insurgent Terrorism" (original source: A. P. Schmid and J. de Graaf, *Violence as Communication: Insurgent Terrorism and the Western News Media*, Beverly Hills, CA: Sage, 1982, p. 176); and Alex P. Schmid, "Frameworks for Conceptualizing Terrorism," *Terrorism and Political Violence*, Vol. 16, No. 2, Summer 2004, pp. 197-221, esp. "Terrorism as/and Communication," pp. 205-210. The key role of mass media in transmitting terrorist signals explains how "deeds themselves," if propagated like waves beyond their initial victims to the ultimate target, is the focus here.

It is this mediated function then that permits terror to function as tactic and political strategy. See also Thomas Perry Thornton, "Terror as a Weapon of Political Agitation," Harry Eckstein, ed., *Internal War: Problems and Approaches*, New York, The Free Press, 1964, pp. 71-99; Ronald D. Crelinsten, "Analysing Terrorism and Counter-Terrorism: A Communication Model," *Terrorism and Political Violence*, 2002, Vol. 14, No. 2, pp. 77-122; Andrew H. Kydd and Barbara F. Walter, "The Strategies of Terrorism," *International Security*, 2006, Vol. 31, No. 1, pp. 49-80; Ariel Merari, "Terrorism as a Strategy of Insurgency," *Terrorism and Political Violence*, 1993, Vol. 5, No. 4, pp. 213-251. For the original formulations of the notion "propaganda of the deed," see John Most, "Advice for Terrorists," (orig. in *Freiheit*, September 13, 1884), "Action as Propaganda," Walter Laqueur and Yohah Alexander, eds., *The Terrorism Reader*, New York: Meridian, pp. 100-108, especially Part III, "Action as Propaganda," pp. 105-106.

155. A recent "controversy" involving Bruce Hoffman and Marc Sageman led, in my opinion, to a false dichotomy; that radicalization and recruitment is **either** exclusively top-down (Hoffman) **or** exclusively via the emergence of self-radicalizers and home-based and home-grown persons primarily initially morally outraged by AQ propaganda or personal or vicarious identification with other's humiliation and suffering. For these overly-polarized positions, see Bruce Hoffman, "The Myth of Grass-Roots Terrorism: Why Osama bin Laden Still Matters," Review Essay, *Foreign Affairs*, May/June 2008; "The Leaderless Jihad's Leader: Why Osama Bin Laden Mattered," *Foreign Affairs*, May 13, 2011, available from *www.foreignaffairs.com/print/67785*; Bruce Hoffman, "A Counterterrorism Strategy for the Obama Administration," *Terrorism and Political Violence*, 2009, Vol. 21, pp. 359-377. In Hoffman's more recent writings, however, one encounters a more diversified enemy that accommodates varying relations between core, affiliated, and inspired. See, e.g., Peter Bergen, Bruce Hoffman, and Katherine Tiedemann, "Assessing the Jihadist Terrorist Threat to America and American Interests," *Studies in Conflict & Terrorism*, 2011, Vol. 34, pp. 65-101; and Bruce Hoffman, "Al Qaeda's Uncertain Future," *Studies in Conflict and Terrorism*, 2013, Vol. 36, pp. 635-653. For Sageman's position, see Marc Sageman, "Response to Hoffman's Review Essay 'The Myth of Grassroots Terrorism'"; Marc Sageman, "Confronting al-Qaeda: Understanding the Threat in Afghanistan and

Beyond," Testimony to the Senate Foreign Relations Committee, Washington, DC, October 7, 2009, available from *www.foreign. senate.gov/hearings/confronting-al-Qaeda-understanding-the-threat-in-afghanistan-and-beyond*; reprinted in *Perspectives on Terrorism*, December 2009, Vol. 3, No. 4, pp. 4-25; Rick Maze, "Researcher: Most terrorist plots have no al-Qaida link," *Army Times*, October 19, 2009, p. 14; Marc Sageman, *Understanding Terror Networks*, Philadelphia, PA: University of Pennsylvania Press, 2004; Marc Sageman, *Leaderless Jihad: Terror Networks in the Twenty-First Century*, Philadelphia, PA: University of Pennsylvania Press, 2009.

156. Sageman, *Leaderless Jihad*, pp. viii, 3, 11, 13, 22, 24, 25, 143-146.

157. See, for examples, Colonel G. L. Lamborn, USAR (Ret.), "Jihad of the Pen: A Practioners Guide to Conducting Effective Influence Operations in an Insurgency," *Small Wars Journal*, February 2010, 122 pp., esp. pp. 67-72, available from *www.smallwarsjournal.com*; Christian Clai and Major Marc Romanych, USA (Retired), "Counterpropaganda: An Important Capability for Joint Forces," *IO Sphere*, Fall 2005, pp. 11-13; Michael Egner, "Social Science Foundations for Strategic Communications in the Global War on Terrorism," Paul Davis and Kim Cragin, eds., *Social Science for Counterterrorism: Putting the Pieces Together*, Santa Monica, CA: The RAND Corporation, 2009, Chap. 9, pp. 323-365, esp. pp. 327-330; Colonel W. C. Garrison, "Information Operations and Counter-Propaganda: Making a Weapon of Public Affairs," Strategy Research Project, Carlisle, PA: U.S. Army War College, March 17, 1999; Cori E. Dauber, "The TRUTH is out there: Responding to Insurgent Disinformation and Deception Operations," *Military Review*, January-February 2009, pp. 13-24; Todd Leventhal, *Iraqi Propaganda and Disinformation During the Gulf War: Lessons for the Future*, The Emirates Occasional Papers, No. 36, Abu Dhabi, UAE: The Emirates Center for Strategic Studies and Research, 1999; Droukje Demant and Beatrice De Graaf, "How to Counter Radical Narratives: Dutch Deradicalization Policy in the Case of Moluccan and Islamic Radicals," *Studies in Conflict and Terrorism*, Vol. 33, 2010, pp. 408-428; Beatrice de Graaf, "Counter-Narratives and the Unrehearsed Stories Counter-Terrorists Unwittingly Produce," *Perspectives on Terrorism*, August 2009, Vol. 3, No. 2, pp. 5-11; Larisa Breton and Adam Pearson, "Contextual Truth-Telling to Counter Extremist-Supportive Mes-

saging Online: The Wikileaks 'Collateral Murder' Case Study, *Small Wars Journal*, November 6, 2010, available from *www.small-warsjournal.com*; Nancy Snow, "Public Diplomacy and Propaganda: Rethinking Diplomacy in the Age of Persuasion," December 4, 2012; See also Leonard W. Doob, "Goebbels' Principles of Propaganda," *The Public Opinion Quarterly*, Vol. 14, No. 3, Autumn 1950, pp. 419-442, esp. p. 441, for the critical observation that no matter how masterful the propagandist, facts can be very troublesome things. Doob states, for example:

> Goebbels clearly recognized his own propaganda impotency in six situations. The basic drives of sex and hunger were not appreciably affected by propaganda. Air raids brought the problems ranging from discomfort to death which could not be gainsaid. Propaganda could not significantly increase industrial production. The religious impulses of many Germans and by peoples of the occupied countries required forceful action, not clever words. Finally, Germany's unfavorable military situation became an undeniable fact. When propaganda and censorship could not be effective, Goebbels advocated action or, in one of his official positions . . . he himself produced the action. Diversionary propaganda he considered second-best.

158. The terms "Psychological Operations" and "PSYOPS" are entirely deleted from JP 1-02.

159. *Field Manual (FM) 3-05.130, Army Special Operations Forces Unconventional Warfare*, Washington, DC: DoD, September 2008, p. 4-14, para 4-74.

160. *Information Operations Primer*, p. 4.

161. JP 3-13.2.

162. This essential function and its potential evacuation or confusion in the term, Military Information Support Operations and its acronym MISO led to spirited debate among PSYOP personnel. See, for example, Alfred Paddock, Jr., "PSYOP: On a Complete Change in Organization, Practice, and Doctrine," *Small Wars Journal*, June 2010; Alfred E. Paddock, "Legitimizing Army Psychological Operations," *Joint Forces Quarterly*, Issue 56, 1st Quarter, 2010, pp. 89-93; See Lawrence Dietz, "MISO: Is it Soup Yet?"

available from *psyopregiment.blogspot.com/2010/06/miso-is-it-soup-yet.html* and its many replies; "Psyop expert discusses military information support operations," Washington, DC: The Institute of World Politics, March 9, 2011, available from *www.iwp.edu/news_publications/detail/psyop-expert-discusses-military-information-support-operations*; Kevin Maurer, "Psychological Operations are now Military Information Support Operations," Associated Press, July 2, 2010, available from *publicintelligence.net/psychological-operations-are-now-military-information-support-operations/*; and more generally, from *www.psywarrior.com*.

163. See, for example, Kelton Rhoads, *Introduction to Influence*, 1997-2012, *Working Psychology*, available from *www.workingpsychology.com*; Eric V. Larson, Richard E. Darilek, Daniel Gibran, Brian Nichiporuk, Amy Richardson, Lowell H. Schwartz, and Cathryn Q. Thurston, *Foundations of Effective Influence Operations: A Framework for Enhancing Army Capabilities*, Santa Monica, CA: The RAND Corporation, 2009, esp. p. xiii, 1-7, for influence operations broadly and counterpropaganda, and p. 6, for critical significance of actions; Lieutenant Colonel Susan L. Gough, "The Evolution of Strategic Influence," Strategy Research Project, April 7, 2003, Carlisle, PA: U.S. Army War College, p.1, for definition of strategic influence, and pp. 8, 9, 29, esp. 30-37, for role of counterpropaganda; Kim Cragin and Scott Gerwehr, *Dissuading Terror: Strategic Influence and the Struggle Against Terrorism*, Santa Monica, CA: The RAND Corporation, 2005; Paul K. Davis, *Simple Models to Explore Deterrence and More General Influence in the War with al-Qaeda*, Santa Monica, CA: The RAND Corporation, 2010; Alex S. Wilner, "Deterring the Undeterrable: Coercion, Denial, and Delegitimation in Counterterrorism," Amos Perlmutter Prize Essay, *The Journal of Strategic Studies*, February 2011, Vol. 34, No. 1, pp. 3-37; Dr. Lee Rowland and Commander Steve Tatham, RN, "Strategic Communication & Influence Operations: Do We Really Get 'It'?," *www.smallwarsjournal.com*, August 3, 2010; "Influence Operations," Maxwell Air Force Base, AL: Air University, Cyberspace & Information Study Center, available from *www.au.af.mil/info-ops/influence.htm*; Major Roy P. Fatur, USAF, "Influencing Transnational Terrorist Organizations: Using Influence Nets to Prioritize Factors," June 2005, Graduate Research Project, Maxwell Air Force Base, AL: Air University, Air Force Institute of Technology.

164. See Qiao Liang and Wang Xiangsui, *Unrestricted Warfare*, Beijing, China: PLA Literature and Arts Publishing House, February 1999, esp. pp. 51-56, and 191-194, for conceptions of methods and means, and their infinite combinations, extending well beyond those traditionally conceived; Foreign Broadcast Information Service (FBIS) Partial translation.

165. Cheng Hang Teo, Major, Republic of Singapore Air Force, *The Acme of Skill: Nonkinetic Warfare*, Wright Flyer Paper No. 30, Maxwell Air Force Base, AL: Air Command and Staff College, May 2008, p. 1.

166. Qiao Liang and Wang Xiangsui, *Unrestricted Warfare*, esp. pp. 56-57; See also esp. pp. 7, 12, 50-57, 56-57, 115, endnotes #27-#29, pp. 112-113; 117, 119-120, 128-129, 168-69, 180-181, 216, and 221. See also Major Michael J. Good, USA, *Chinese National Strategy of Total War*, Maxwell Air Force Base, AL: Air University, Air Force Institute of Technology, June 2008, in partial fulfillment for the Degree of Master of Science in Cyber Warfare, Wright-Patterson Air Force Base, OH, see esp. pp. 3-12 on doctrine of total war—war across all domains and battlefields from Sun Tzu, Mao, Deng Xiaoping, and others; pp. 13-33, esp. p. 28 for battlefields/conduct of total war; pp. 34-48, Cyber Space in the Total War; and, Conclusions, pp. 49-53, available from *handle.dtic.mil/100.2/ADA487635*. See also James R. Clapper, Director of National Intelligence, in recent Congressional testimony, states:

> This year [2013], in both content and organization, . . . illustrates how quickly and radically the world—and our threat environment—are changing. The environment is demanding reevaluations of the way we do business, expanding our analytic envelope, and altering the vocabulary of intelligence. Threats are more diverse, interconnected, and viral than at any time in history. Attacks, which might involve cyber and financial weapons, can be deniable and unattributable. Destruction can be invisible, latent, and progressive (see also esp. pp. 1-3, analyzing the cyber domain).

Statement for the Record, Worldwide Threat Assessment of the US Intelligence Community, House Permanent Select Committee on Intelligence, Washington, DC.

167. See, for example, *Field Manual (FM) 3-05.130, Army Special Forces Unconventional Warfare*, September 2008, Washington, DC: Department of the Army, pp. 2-1 to 2-11, available from *www.us.army.mil*. See also Colonel Jack D. Kem (Retired), "Understanding the operational environment: the expansion of DIME,"*Military Intelligence Professional Bulletin* (MIPB), April-June 2007, Vol. 33, No. 2, pp. 49-53, for a history of the coinage of DIME, DIMEFIL (or MIDLIFE), and uneven adoption of the latter in various relatively recent publications.

168. Even and Siman-Tov, conceptualize cyberspace thusly:

> The term 'cyberspace' defines a phenomenon that emerged with the invention of the telegraph in 1844, which involves taking advantage of the electromagnetic field for human needs by means of technology. An essential turning point in the development of cyberspace was the invention of the numerical computer in 1949. Other milestones include: the linking of communications networks with computers and machines, which began in the 1970s; mass use of the internet and personal computers since the mid-1990s; and in the past decade, the comprehensive integration between computer systems and various communications systems and machines (such as in industry, transportation, and other fields), the mass use of handheld cellular devices, the flourishing of social networks on the internet, and more. All of these have profoundly influenced society and the economy. Information technologies and cyberspace are rapidly changing the nature of the modern battlefield as well.

Cyber Warfare: Concepts and Strategic Trends, Memorandum 117, Tel Aviv, Israel: INSS, May 2012, p. 9, available from *www.inss.org.il*.

169. For example, for select press reporting existence of a cyber warfare doctrine, see Max Fisher, "Leaked documents hint at Obama's emerging cyberwar doctrine," *The Washington Post*, June 7, 2013, available from *www.washingtonpost.com/blogs*; Robert O'Harrow, Jr., and Barton Gellman, "Secret cyber directive calls for ability to attack without warning," *The Washington Post*, June 7, 2013, available from *www.washingtonpost.com*; Cheryl Pellerin, "Cybercom Builds Teams for Offense, Defense in Cyberspace," Washington, DC: DoD, March 12, 2013, available from

www.defense.gov; Ellen Nakashima, "Pentagon creating teams to launch cyberattacks as threat grows," *The Washington Post*, March 12, 2013, available from *www.washingtonpost.com*; Jim Garamone, "Clapper Places Cyber at Top of Transnational Threat List," Washington, DC: DoD, March 12, 2013, available from *www.defense.gov*; Dave Tolikar, "At Nellis AFB, teaching the shadowy art of cyber warfare," *Stars & Stripes*, available from *www.stripes.com*; Jim Garamone, "NSA Chief: Cyber World Presents Opportunities, Challenges," Washington, DC: DoD, available from *www.defense.gov*. For select reports and analyses on various dimensions of cyberspace as a warfare domain, see *Department of Defense Strategy for Operating in Cyberspace*, Washington, DC: DoD, July 2011, available from *www.defense.gov/news/d20110714cyber.pdf*; Joseph S. Nye, Jr., *Cyber Power*, Cambridge, MA: Harvard Kennedy School, Belfer Center for Science and International Affairs, May 2010, available from *belfercenter.ksg.harvard.edu_files/cyber_power.pdf*; Jon Brickey, Jacob Cox, John Nelson, and Gregory Conti, "The Case for Cyber," *Small Wars Journal*, available from *smallwarsjournal.com/print/13223*; Gary D. Brown and Owen W. Tullos, "On the Spectrum of Cyberspace Operations," *Small Wars Journal*, available from *smallwarsjournal.com/print/13595*; Michael N. Schmitt, "International Law in Cyberspace: The Koh Speech and Tallinn Manual Juxtaposed," *Harvard International Law Journal*, Vol. 54, December 2012, pp. 13-37; "The Tallin Manual on the International Law Applicable to Cyber Warfare," Tallinn, Estonia: NATO Cooperative Cyber Defence Centre of Excellence, available from *www.ccdcoe.org/249.html*.

170. A possible mnemonic device is suggested in the following ordering and pronunciation of this eight-fold concept: DICE-FILM (pronounced, "Dicey Film").

171. See, for example, John J. Mearsheimer and Stephen M. Walt, *The Israel Lobby and U.S. Foreign Policy*, New York, Farrar, Straus and Giroux, 2007.

172. This methodology is presently pursued by the Center for Strategic Counterterrorism Communications (CSCC), subordinate to the Under Secretary for Public Diplomacy and Public Affairs but, in fact, an interagency enterprise involving key elements of the national security and intelligence communities. A brief summation of its activities is provided by Jo Becker and Scott Shane,

"Secret 'Kill List' Proves a Test of Obama's Principles and Will," *The New York Times*, in which the authors report: "a sophisticated, interagency war room at the State Department to counter the jihadi narrative on an hour-by-hour basis, posting messages and video online and providing talking points to embassies." Consisting primarily of a re-purposed digital engagement team initially tasked to the State Department's Bureau of Counterterrorism, their mission is to enter terrorist venues, and comprised of a small pool of personnel fluent in Arabic, Farsi, Urdu, and Somali, seek to undermine AQ propaganda. For USG policy and enabling legislation, see USAID, *Leading Through Civilian Power: The First Quadrennial Diplomacy and Development Review* (QDDR), Washington, DC, 2010, Chap. 2, Adapting to the Diplomatic Landscape of the 21st Century, III. Engaging Beyond the State, 1. Public Diplomacy, Shape the Narrative, Expand and strengthen people-to-people relationships, (p. 62) Counter violent extremism, "Creating a Center for Counterterrorism Communications," available from *www.state.gov/s/dmr/qddr/*; Office of the President of the United States, Executive Order # 13584, *Developing an Integrated Strategic Counterterrorism Communications Initiative and Establishing a Temporary Organization to Support Certain Government-Wide Communications Activities Directed Abroad*, Washington, DC: The White House, September 9, 2011; Office of the President of the United States, *Update to Congress on National Framework for Strategic Communication*, Washington, DC: The White House, 2012, available from *www.hsdl.org/?view&did=704809*, in which the President defines the Center for Strategic Counterterrorism Communications' (CSCC's) three foci: "confronting al-Qa'ida rhetoric through direct digital engagement . . . providing tools for United States Government communicators; and working with specific U.S. Embassies' country teams to develop plans for engagement at the local level" (pp. 6-7); U.S. Department of State, "Center for Strategic Communications," Washington, DC: Department of State, available from *www.state.gov/r/cscc/*; Richard LeBaron, "The State Department's Role in Countering Violent Extremism," Prepared Remarks [only a portion of the forum that was on the record], Policy Focus 119, Washington, DC: The Washington Institute for Near East Policy, November 18, 2011; Richard LeBaron, "Public Diplomacy as an Instrument of Counterterrorism: A Progress Report," Speech, President's Round Table, Diplomatic and Consular Officers Retired (DACOR), Washington, DC, DACOR Bacon House, June 20, 2012; "Communicating with Terror: A Briefing and Discussion with the

Center for Strategic Counterterrorism Communications," Atlantic Council; "Ambassador Alberto Fernandez Appointed Coordinator of the CSCC, Washington, DC: U.S. Department of State, March 26, 2012; U. S. House of Representatives, Hearing Before the Subcommittee on Terrorism, Nonproliferation, and Trade of the Committee on Foreign Affairs, *The State Department's Center for Strategic Counterterrorism Communications: Mission, Operations and Impact*, Washington, DC: House of Representatives, 112th Cong., Second Sess., Serial No. 112-164, August 2, 2012, available from *www.foreignaffairs.house.gov/*; Ambassador Alberto M. Fernandez, *Statement of Ambassador Alberto M. Fernandez, Coordinator for the Center of Strategic Counterterrorism Communications before the House Foreign Affairs Subcommittee on Terrorism, Nonproliferation and Trade*, Washington, DC: August 2, 2012; For press accounts and commentary, see "State, SOCOM Partner to Counter Cyberterrorism," Stony Brook, NY: The Simons Center, June 6, 2012, available from *thesimonscenter.org/state-socom-partner-to-counter-cyberterrorism/*; Philip Palin, "Text, subtext, and terrorism," *Homeland Security Watch*, July 15, 2011; Helle C. Dale, "WebMemo," No. 3348, August 31, 2011, "Congress Must Set High Bar for White House Strategic Communications Plan," available from *report. heritage.org/wm3348*; Philip Ewing, Dod Buzz, "U.S. rolls out new counter-terror comms plan," September 9, 2011, available from *www.dodbuzz.com/2011/09/09/u-s-rolls-out-new-counter-terror-comms-plan/*; Helle Dale, "U.S. Counterterrorism Strategy: Sticks and Carrots," Washington, DC: The Heritage Organization, September 15, 2011; Shaun Waterman, "Social networks used to counter al Qaeda: Team tries to impede jihadi recruiters," *Washington Times*, October 5, 2011, available from *www.washingtontimes.com/news/2011/oct/5/social-networks-used-to-counter-al-qaeda*; Camille Elhassani, "US state department fights al-Qaeda in cyberspace," May 25, 2012, available from *blogs.aljazeera.com/blog/Americas/us-state-department-fights-al-qaeda-cyberspace*; Vivian Wagner, "US Cybercounterterrorism Team Takes on al-Qaida," *TechNewsWorld*, May 29, 2012, available from *www.technewsworld.com/story/75238. html*; Judith McHale and Richard LeBaron, "Digitally dissuading tomorrow's terrorists," available from *dyn.politico.com*. The CSCC, though interagency, coordinates and is in direct communication with the Counter Terrorism Bureau in the Department of State (previously the Counter Terrorism Office, and Coordinator for Counter Terrorism). See Organization of the Bureau of Counterterrorism, Washington, DC: U.S. Department of State, Washington, DC: U.S. Department of State, available from *www.state. gov/j/ct/about/index.htm*; Daniel Benjamin, Coordinator, Office of the Coordinator for Counterterrorism, "Al-Qaida after Bin Laden," Remarks at the Jamestown Conference at the National Press Club, Jamestown, VA, December 8, 2011, available from *www. state.gov/j/ct/rls/rm/2011/178499.htm*; Daniel Benjamin, Coordinator, Office of the Coordinator for Counterterrorism, "Countering Violent Extremism," Remarks at the Near East/South Asia Center for Strategic Studies (NESA), Washington, DC: Near East/South Asia Center for Strategic Studies, January 25, 2012, available from *www.state.gov/j/ct/rls/rm/2012/182716.htm*; Daniel Benjamin, Coordinator, Office of the Coordinator for Counterterrorism, "The State Department's Bureau of Counterterrorism: Budget, Programs, and Policies," Testimony before House Foreign Affairs Committeee Subcommittee on Terrorism, Nonproliferation, and Trade," Washington, DC: U.S. House of Representations, April 18, 2012, available from *www.state.gov/j/ct/rls/rm/2012/188815. htm*; Daniel Benjamin, Coordinator, Bureau of Counterterrorism, "Global Counterterrorism: A Progress Report," Remarks, Washington, DC, Brookings Institution, December 18, 2012, available from *www.state.gov/j/ct/rls/rm/2012/202179.htm*.

173. For a brief discussion identifying these three bases of a counteroffensive, see Omar Ashour, "Online De-Radicalization? Countering Violent Extremist Narratives: Message, Messenger, and Media Strategy," *Perspectives on Terrorism*, Vol. 4, No. 6, December 2010, pp. 15-19.

174. For Osama bin Ladin's tactical propaganda during the 1994-2004 period, see especially, FBIS Report, *Compilation of Usama bin Ladin Statements, 1994-January 2004*, January 2004, available from *www.fas.org/irp/world/para/ubl-fbis.pdf*. For a recent compilation that includes the above source but covers the time frame 1991-2009 and also includes Dr. Ayman al-Zawahiri's propaganda, see Donald Holbrook, "Al-Qaeda Communiques by Bin Laden and Al-Zawahiri: A Chronology," Alex P. Schmid, *The Routledge Handbook of Terrorism Research*, London, UK, and New York: Routledge, 2011/2013, "Appendix 4.3," pp. 280-293.

175. For a very insightful analysis of this process of fabrications becoming signifiers and legends, and the means of preventing that, see Beatrice de Graaf, "Counter-Narratives and the

Unrehearsed Stories Counter-Terrorists Unwittingly Produce,"
Perspectives on Terrorism, Vol. 3, No. 2, August 2009, pp. 5-11;
Froukje Demant and Beatrice De Graaf, "How to Counter Radical
Narratives: Dutch Deradicalization Policy in the Case of Moluc-
can and Islamic Radicals," *Studies in Conflict and Terrorism*, Vol. 33,
2010, pp. 408-428.

176. See, for example, Robert D. Benford and David A. Snow,
"Framing Processes and Social Movements," *Annual Review of Sociology*, Vol. 26, 2000, pp. 611-639.

177. This very accurately describes U.S. attempts, repeated
over many years both in public (i.e., the UN Security Council,
UN General Assembly), or in private communiques among State
Department embassy and intelligence officials, to prevent Osama
Bin Laden from using Taliban-controlled territory to issue declarations of war against America and Americans; train terrorists
targeting the U.S. homeland; and after the 1998 embassy bombings in Kenya and Tanzania, the issuing of a federal indictment
(*United States v. Usama bin Laden et al.*, S(2) 98 Cr. 1023 (LBS)
(S.D.N.Y. Nov. 4, 1998) to avoid extradition to the United States
to face the criminal justice system. See, for example, the following
UN Security Council Resolutions (S.C. Res. 1189 (1998), August
13, 1998; S.C. Res. 1193 (1998), August 28, 1998; S.C. Res.s 1214
(1998), December 8, 1998; S/1999/1021, October 4, 1999: "Letter
dated 1 October 1999 from the Deputy Permanent Representative
of the United States of America to the United Nations Addressed
to the Secretary-General" S.C. Res. 1267 (1999), October 15 1999).
These contain explicit references to the Taliban as facilitating the
AQ terrorist sanctuary. There was unanimity on every resolution
listed above except for a single vote involving two abstentions.
Additional pre-9/11 resolutions include: S.C. Res. 1333 (2000),
December 19, 2000; S/2001/511, May 22, 2001, which includes
[1] "Letter dated 21 May from Secretary-General addressed to the
President of the Security Council." [Re: Committee of Experts to
report on how arms embargo and terrorist training camp closure
would be monitored and enforced.] and, [2] "Letter dated May
18, 2001, from the Chairman of the Committee of Experts on Afghanistan appointed pursuant to Security Council resolution 1333
(2000) addressed to the Secretary-General," whose "Enclosure" is:
"Report of the Committee of Experts appointed pursuant to Security Resolution 1333 (2000), para. 15 (a), regarding monitoring of

the arms embargo against the Taliban and the closure of terrorist training camps in the Taliban-held areas of Afghanistan"; and S.C. Res. 1363 (2001), July 30, 2001, the last pre-9/11 attempt to have the Taliban extradite bin Laden, eliminate terrorist sanctuary, and end the flow of materials, weapons, and monies to AQ. Further corroboration of the extensive efforts to which the USG went during the period 1994-2001 to negotiate secretly with high-level Taliban for extradition of Osama bin Laden and elimination of terrorist sanctuaries, may be found at The National Security Archive, available from *www.gwu.edu/~nsarchiv*. Here are two notable examples from among dozens of documents. Following the USG launching of cruise missiles against Khost in Afghanistan and Khartoum, Sudan in response to Bin Laden's bombing of the East African Embassies, on August 22, 1998, Mullah Omar called a State Department official. (See *www.gwu.edu/~nsarchiv/NSAEBB/NSAEBB134/Doc%202.pdf.*) The subject heading of this document: "Afghanistan: Taliban's Mullah Omar's 8/22 Contact with State Department." A Summary of the 4-page Cable is furnished (capitalization in original):

TALIBAN SUPREME LEADER MULLAH OMAR TOLD A STATE DEPARTMENT OFFICIAL IN WASHINGTON THAT THE TALIBAN WAS OPEN TO THE SUGGESTION OF ESTABLISHING A VEHICLE FOR SECURE COMMUNICATION WITH USG OFFICIALS, POSSIBLY THROUGH AMEMBASSY ISLAMABAD. WHILE OMAR PARROTED SOME OF BIN LADEN'S HARD-LINE VIEWS, HE LISTENED TO U.S. ARGUMENTS ON THE REASONS FOR U.S. ATTACKS IN AFGHANISTAN AND SUDAN AND THE REASONS WHY BIN LADEN'S CONTINUED ACTIVITIES WERE NOT IN THE INTEREST OF THE AFGHAN PEOPLE. OMAR WARNED THAT THE U.S. STRIKES WOULD PROVE COUNTER-PRODUCTIVE AND AROUSE ANTI-AMERICAN FEELINGS IN THE ISLAMIC WORLD. WHILE HE WAS IN NO WAY THREATENING, HE CLAIMED THE STRIKES COULD SPARK MORE TERRORIST ATTACKS. HE ASKED FOR EVIDENCE OF BIN LADEN'S INVOLVEMENT IN TERRORIST ACTIONS. END SUMMARY.

Though the above cable asserts that plenty of evidence exists of bin Laden's terrorist activities, a follow-up cable on August 23, 1998, see *www.gwu.edu/~nsarchiv/NSAEBB/NSAEBB134/Doc*

%*203.pdf*, which provides the extensive, explicit case listing this evidence, as well as other talking points to be used in follow-up communication. The Subject of this embassy cable dated August 23, 1998, "Message to the Taliban on Bin Laden," is summarized in its first paragraph:

> FOLLOWING UP ON TELEPHONE CONVERSATION WITH TALIBAN LEADER MULLAH OMAR (REFTEL) WHICH INDICATED AN APPARENT OPENNESS FOR DIALOGUE, POST IS INSTRUCTED TO ENGAGE WITH AN AUTHORITATIVE REPRESENTATIVE OF THE TALIBAN TO EXPEL SAUDI TERRORIST OSAMA BIN LADEN SO THAT HE CAN BE PROPERLY BROUGHT TO JUSTICE FOR HIS TERRORIST ACTS. THE APPARENT READINESS OF THE TALIBAN FOR SERIOUS DIALOGUE NEEDS TO BE PROBED, WITH THE REALIZATION THAT IT COULD TURN OUT TO BE A PLOY FOR RECOGNITION OR OTHER BENEFITS OR A DEVICE TO STALL FOR TIME.

For the legality of the U.S. use of force after 9/11 in Operation ENDURING FREEDOM, see *Authorization for Use of Military Force* (AUMF), Public Law No. 107-40, 115 Stat. 224, 2001; The UN Charter, which according to Schmitt (Michael N. Schmitt, *Counter-Terrorism and the Use of Force in International Law*, The Marshall Center Papers, No. 5. Garmisch-Partenkirchen, Germany: The George Marshall Center, 2002, pp. iv + 98), "The Charter in limiting state behavior — Article 2(4) — also empowers states to defend themselves, and this defense is not restricted to defense against state actors (see esp. Article 39, and Article 51)." Was it legal? Schmitt states: "No voices were raised [in the UN Council] claiming that either the customary right of self-defense or Article 51 was limited to the context of State actions" (p. 27). Also consider: NATO's invocation of Article V requiring collective self-defense, the actions of most states, and the fact that "in no case, was there any suggestion that the right was dependent on identifying a State as the attacker" (*Ibid.*), and that post-October 7 United Nations Security Council (UNSC) resolutions "went so far as to urge member States to 'root out terrorism, in keeping with the Charter of the United Nations'" (p.27; see S.C. Res. 1378 (Nov. 14, 2002); S.C. Res. 1386 (Dec. 20, 2001; S.C. Res. 1390 (January 16, 2002); See also S.C. Res. 1368 (September 12, 2001), S.C. Res. 1373 (September 28, 2001), and S.C. Res. 1377 (November 12, 2001).

178. Above excerpts are translated from their Arabic book, *Islam and the Laws of War*, which appeared in serial form in the newspaper, *Al-Sharq Al-Awsat* (London, UK), August-September 2006; Translated and exerpted in MEMRI, "Al-Gama'a Al-Islamiyya vs. Al-Qaeda," available from *www.memri.org/report/en/print1887.htm*.

179. This paraphrase of Isam al-Din Dirbalah, *Istratijiyat wa Tafjirat al-Qa'ida: al-Akhta wa al-Akhtar* (*The al-Qa'ida Organization's Strategy and Bombings: Mistakes and Rulings*), Cairo, Egypt: Maktabat al-Turath al-Islami, 2003, appears in Abd-al-Latif al-Minawi, "Part 1 of Book Review: Egyptian Islamist Leaders Fault Al-Qaida's Strategy," available from *www.opensource.gov*; Original Arabic publication in *Al-Sharq al-Awsat*, Internet Version, January, 11, 2004.

180. See *Ibid.*, for a more expansive discussion of these three phases, presenting very illuminating insights into the Islamic Group's nuanced and objective analysis of U.S. vital interests and policies. With respect to U.S. policies toward Israel and Arab and Muslim issues, it states:

We should not disregard the role of the fundamentalist Christian right in the United States that began to grow and influence the internal and external trends of the Administration. An alliance emerged between the Jewish lobby and the fundamentalist Christian right. The influence of this alliance focused on the Arab-Israeli conflict and found a pretext to meddle in the internal affairs of various countries, especially Muslim countries, under the slogan of 'backing the persecuted minorities in the world'.

The importance of the Islamic Group's rejection of conspiracy theories for explaining the present predicament confronting the Arab and Muslim world is also telling. They state

The conspiracy theory truly means leaving one's [free] will so that only the will of the CIA and the Mossad prevail. Then we blame our mistakes and apathy on the United States, the Israeli conspiracy, and other states, as if we had no role in everything that happened in this world.

(See Najih Ibrahim, Egyptian Group *shura* council member's submitted conference paper, translated and reported in "Egypt: Statement by Leading Islamic Group Figure Says No-Violence Initiative Strong," available from *www.opensource.gov*, original in Arabic, *Al-Misri Al-Yawm*, Cairo, July 2, 2007.)

181. Jihad—striving/struggling in the path of Allah to raise Allah's Word supreme—is classically understood to take five forms: jihad of the heart/soul, designed to cleanse one of impure intentions and thoughts (*jihad bil nafs/qalb*), jihad of the tongue (*jihad bil lisan*), jihad of the pen/knowledge (*jihad bil qalam/ilm*), jihad of the hand, i.e., commanding the good and forbidding the bad through bodily reward and punishment (*jihad bil yad*), and the most potentially life-threatening and therefore most regulated of all, the jihad of the sword (*jihad bis saif*).

182. The words we use to describe AQ's actions are key to their legal and moral status in Islam. For an important contribution to leveraging Islamic law and morality to further marginalize and criminalize AQ, see "Words that Work and Words that Don't: A Guide for Counterterrorism Communication," Vol. 2, No. 10, McLean, VA: National Counter Terrorism Center, Counterterrorism Communications Center, March 14, 2008, p. 14, available from *www.investigativeproject.org/documents/misc/127.pdf*; Office for Civil Rights and Civil Liberties, *Terminology to Define the Terrorists: Recommendations from American Muslims*, Washington, DC: U.S. Department of Homeland Security, January 2008, available from *www.dhs.gov/terminology-define-terrorists-recommendations-american-muslims*. The words we use to describe our "war" against the AQ terrorist entity are also telling. For a remarkably wise and prescient, early post-9/11 reflection by a noted military historian and theorist, see Michael Howard, Comment: "What's in a Name?: How to Fight Terrorism," *Foreign Affairs*, January/February 2002 (based on a London lecture given October 30, 2001), available from *www.foreignaffairs.com/print/57615*.

183. See Kamolnick, *Delegitimizing Al-Qaeda*; Paul Kamolnick, "Al Qaeda's *Sharia* Crisis: Sayyid Imam and the Jurisprudence of Lawful Military Jihad" (for former Al Qaeda shari'a guide, Sayyid Imam's comprehensive fiqh-based critique of AQ's doctrine of 'killing in masse'); and Kamolnick, "The Egyptian Islamic Group's Critique of Al Qaeda's Interpretation of Jihad."

184. *Ibid.*

185. For an examination of several key moral objections to terrorism, particularly its parasitic nature as a form of moral free-riding, see Paul Kamolnick, "Defending Liberal Democracy in an Age of Terror," *Terrorism and Political Violence*, 2012, Vol. 24, esp. pp. 148-157.

186. Amaney A. Jamal, "It's Not Who We Are, It's What We Do," *Foreign Affairs*, Vol. 92, No. 5, September/October 2013, pp. 152-154.

187. *Ibid.* p. 154.

188. See especially Harry R. Yarger, *Strategic Theory for the 21st Century: The Little Book on Big Strategy*, Carlisle, PA: Strategic Studies Institute, U.S. Army War College, February 2006, available from *www.StrategicStudiesInstitute.army.mil*; H. Richard Yarger, "Toward a Theory of Strategy: Art Lykke and the U.S. Army War College Strategy Model," J. Boone Bartholomees, Jr., ed., *U.S. Army War College Guide to National Security Issues, Vol. I: Theory of War and Strategy*, 5th Ed., Carlisle, PA: Strategic Studies Institute, U.S. Army War College, June 2012, pp. 45-51; Appendix I, "Guidelines for Strategy Formulation," pp. 413-418, J. Boone Bartholomees, Jr., ed., *U.S. Army War College Guide to National Security Issues, Vol. II: National Security Policy and Strategy*, 5th Ed., Carlisle, PA: Strategic Studies Institute, U.S. Army War College, June 2012; Arthur F. Lykke, Jr., "Chap. 13: Toward an Understanding of Military Strategy," J. R. Cerami and J. F. Holcomb, Jr., eds., *U.S. Army War College Guide to Strategy*, Carlisle, PA: Strategic Studies Institute, U.S. Army War College, February 2001. pp. 179-185.

www.ingramcontent.com/pod-product-compliance
Lightning Source LLC
Chambersburg PA
CBHW071355280526
45787CB00001B/337